MYTHS
OF THE
DREAMING

INTERPRETING
ABORIGINAL LEGENDS

JAMES G. COWAN

PRISM PRESS

'For Jill Ker Conway, *eruditus*'

Published in Great Britain 1994 by

PRISM PRESS
2 South Street,
Bridport,
Dorset DT6 3NQ

Distributed in the USA by

THE ATRIUM PUBLISHERS GROUP,
PO BOX 108,
Lower Lake
CA 95157

Published in Australia by

UNITY PRESS
P.O. Box 480,
Roseville NSW 2069

ISBN 1 85327 085 7

© 1994 James G. Cowan

Typeset by Prism Press, Bridport, Dorset.

Printed by The Guernsey Press ltd,
The Channel Islands.

Contents

Introduction

At a recent international congress on rock art held in Cairns, Australia, evidence was introduced to suggest that Australia, not Europe nor Africa, was home to the oldest known art, culture, and possibly even language. Research conducted at three sites in north-eastern South Australia pointed to the existence of a cultural and artistic tradition reaching back 44,000 years. These pre-dated the earliest European cave art sites by some five to ten thousand years. Furthermore this date challenged the dominant view that art, language, and culture developed for the first time in Western Europe. Whoever the first inhabitants of Australia were they already possessed stone tool technology, and almost certainly sophisticated language and communication skills, all at a time when Europe was still inhabited by Neanderthal Man. Their rock engravings revealed patterns of circles, lines, bird and kangaroo tracks, which suggested that the artists were already familiar with cognitive thought and language.

Such a discovery merely highlights the significance of ancient Australia as a window overlooking the origins of humankind. Here among rocky enclaves, cave galleries, and etched on stony outcrops, were examples of the first flowering of the mythopoeic mind. At some point in history men and women gathered around fires on this vast, empty continent to formulate rituals that accounted for the Creation of the world. Of course, it did not seem like a 'world' to them, but their tribal territory would have embodied a cosmos nonetheless. It was this cosmos that they had chosen to celebrate by way of art, song, dance, and of course in their myths. Only in their myths would they have been able to render the supreme invisibility of primal events in a way that was worthy of their respect and reverence.

My own research among the Aboriginal people of Australia

1

led me to believe that the link with those artists of the past who first made circle patterns on the rocks with their stone implements has not yet been broken. Tribal elders I have met over the years intimated to me that lying embedded in their own myth-life was information which gave account of theirs, and by implication our own origins. These men were heirs to an important tradition, a tradition that reached back into the dim reaches of time. Alone among peoples they possessed the earliest known record that we possess of the sacred history of Creation, and how their forebears had dealt with such knowledge in the first place. In a sense, these Aboriginal elders were the last custodians of a transcendent knowledge which the world now finds itself in danger of losing.

It became obvious that by trying to explore Aboriginal myths in terms of their symbolic significance, it might be possible to lift the veil that has existed for so long over the nature of human spirituality. Could these myths tell us more about what we wanted to know? Were they repositories of hieratic knowledge which might well change the way we think, even today? I had no way of knowing until I had begun the process of analysis, of course. I was always aware that whatever insights emerged from my research, these would always be conditional, since there was no real chance of ever verifying mythopoeic activity, at least not through the use of conventional methods. By its very nature myth defies all our attempts to realize its message objectively. This was not my intent, however. I would be satisfied if I could learn how to understand the language of myth in its universal context, and so begin to converse mythically for the first time. It would be enough to understand the interworld in which my Aboriginal friends had existed for so long, victims not so much of visions or indeed hallucinations, but rather of the august decrees of Dreaming heroes who inhabited that region along with them.

I had always looked upon Aboriginal myths as being too difficult to unravel. They seemed to be too raw, too unstructured in terms of narrative. The Dreaming heroes portrayed in them offered none of the personal characteristics we have come to associate with more modern mythic heroes, whether they be Greek, Egyptian or Indian. There were no Osiris, Apollo, Shiva or Radha to be found parading their exotic identities in their stories. And yet there was something strangely hypnotic about the Dreaming heroes, as if they partook of another reality altogether. Their activities were not so much heroic as prototypal. Their appeal lay less in their invocation of qualities as in their invocation of origins. I was never going to encounter the quixotic nature of a Hermes among these Dreaming heroes, nor discover a Heracles completing his twelve monstrous acts of labour. In fact, it became clear that the personality of many of our so-called 'mythic heroes' had long ago overtaken their true mythic identity and made them appear 'all too human' in our eyes.

The challenge lay in comparing Aboriginal myths with their counterparts in other, more recent traditions in order to uncover correspondences. Aboriginal myths might be shown to embody the true archeology of the spirit as it struggled to give form to its own inherent numinosity. I was interested to discover whether Krishna's dalliance with the milk maids might turn out to be a later version of the Great Snake's consumption of the Wauwalak Sisters, since the principle of the victory of unity over division was implicit in both myths. I wanted to find out whether mythological analogy could help to break down the impenetrability of Aboriginal myths, thus revealing a rich source of sacred knowledge lying beneath the surface of the narrative.

More importantly the prospect of re-vivifying what is by its very nature extremely old cultural material stimulated my endeavour. Years of wandering in the outback of Australia, visiting sacred places in the company of Aboriginal custodians, and listening to old men relating their myths to me as we sat in the shade of cliff overhangs — such memories and experiences made me realize how precious is the knowledge of tribal people. They alone seem to have remained in contact with the primordial forces which fashioned us all. They alone seem to have retained the ability to converse with the spirit of nature in a way that assures them of a role within nature itself. It seemed that mythic identity was important to them as a way of accounting for their origins, for only when relating their myths were they most truly themselves.

The task seemed daunting enough. How was I to overcome my intrinsic resistance to stories unfounded in fact? Only after I had tramped across country steeped in myth did I begin to understand the dynamics of myth itself. *Mythos* does not act upon the imaginative faculties so much as upon a deeper, intuitive thought-process that stems from the soul alone. It performs like a pilot fish, guiding us through the waters of life towards our ultimate destination. Myths are not simply stories; they represent a language of their own. Knowing it was possible to learn this language made me realize that it was also possible to develop that part of one's mind governed by the mythopoeic.

I have my Aboriginal friends to thank for their assistance. They taught me how to 'listen to the land', how to detect the emanations of mytho-history which continue to rise up, even now, from many regions of Australia. Learning how to imbibe mytho-history, as much through the soles of my feet as through my ears, helped make the task a little easier. At least I knew that I had walked over many stories, rested my tired body on many myths, and experienced the invisible presence of many Dreaming heroes during my travels. These were my companions, the company all men must keep on the homeward voyage. My friends had taught me to listen to the land in a spirit of reverence in order that I might realize its message.

The mythic world of the Dreaming finally opened its doors. Interpretation became as important as objective analysis in the understanding of the mythic process. The Dreaming is not a science, and therefore should not be approached as if it were. It must be approached on its own terms, using the language of myth as the only method of discourse. Hopefully this language, once learnt, will make it easier for others to plumb the depths

Introduction

of spirituality that lie within all mythic traditions. For these make up the real treasury of knowledge from which we must draw if we are to restore the balance between humankind and nature.

Finally it must be said that this book does not set out to explore all aspects of Aboriginal spirituality and culture. These have been dealt with in other works*, both by myself and others, which are currently available. But where key ideas intersect with the text I have attempted to explain them for the benefit of those who are not familiar. For those who are already familiar with such concepts as the Dreaming, totemic identity, the Dream journey, sacred power or *djang* as detailed in my earlier books, this work will not be difficult to follow. The myth material, however, does stand alone, and can be understood independently of Aboriginal culture, since it partakes of the Primordial Tradition. Hopefully this tradition will ensure that the mysterious beauty of the Dreaming, as it is portrayed in Aboriginal myths, will be revealed in all its grandeur.

Nor should it be implied that Aboriginal myths pre-date all other world myths. Nonetheless Aboriginal culture does offer us a window overlooking the workings of a Paleolithic tradition, which in itself makes it possible for us to study their myth and belief in the light of more recent cosmologies. This is not to say that other cosmologies stem from those of the Aborigines. My intention has been to emphasise a relationship between them on the plane of cosmogenic belief only. What Aboriginal myths do demonstrate, however, because we still have interpreters and ritual specialists alive today, is the way in which myths work towards the resolution of complex metaphysical ideas. For this reason alone we should be grateful that the Aborigines of Australia have continued to preserve the tradition of the Dreaming for as long as they have.

James G. Cowan
Sydney, 1992
(* see Bibliography)

Part 1:
View from Ankota

CHAPTER 1
Encountering Myth

For many, the desert is often conceived of as a lonely, inhospitable place. A lack of forests, wild animals and great rivers flowing towards a distant ocean means that what lives there does so by dint of its ageless powers of adaptation. Men and animals have learnt how to survive by relying on little but themselves. Yet the desert can also be viewed as a landscape populated not by vast herds of animals grazing as on the veldt, nor by birds flitting through some rainforest canopy, but by a company of mythic creatures that inhabit the invisible terrain of the mind. These feed on our ancestral imagination as surely as rock wallabies do on the scrubby herbage found around waterholes.

In the region of Central Australia known as the Red Centre such a mythic landscape has existed for countless millennia. The homeland of the Aranda, Kukatja, Matutara, Iluara, Walbiri and Wankanura tribes, these peoples have sought to reconcile themselves to an outwardly barren environment by living a rich imaginal life inspired by the power of myth. During the course of untold generations they have drawn up an inner map of the MacDonnell Ranges and the surrounding plains, whereby the outward appearance of the region — its bluffs and gorges, its dry riverbeds and gullies — have become less the representations of certain key landmarks which readily feature on maps, but as 'spirit-marks' pertaining to a wholly otherworldly environment. The Red Centre was, and still is, an endless mythopoem created by the heroes of the Dreaming, that timeless moment when Creation first occurred.

To understand why the Aborigines of Australia invested their homeland with such a mythic dimension is the subject of this book. Prior to the advent of European settlement in 1788, the entire continent was bathed in the afterglow of an age when men and women were content to find the meaning of existence

9

explained to them through their myths. In hindsight it may be said that this age seemed primitive, or that it was hedged in by profound and unremitting ignorance. Men who accepted an invisible reality more completely than they did a material one might themselves be considered as examples of a pre-logical type which had been left over from distant antiquity. Certainly the explorers and pastoralists who came in contact with the Aborigines in the early period of settlement thought so. Reconciling land-use with land-worship was the point at which both parties diverged in the ensuing years of colonization. The process of mythic destruction was indeed relentless. Flocks of sheep and herds of cattle overran the sacred landscape of these mythic heroes, a region that embraced much of inland Australia, reducing it to a vestige of itself. In time the great Dreaming tracks of the ancestral spirits were trampled into non-existence, their sanctuaries abandoned, their telluric power (*kurunba*) utterly diminished.

The destruction of the mythic environment of the Aborigines by its material counterpart in the form of modern agrarian and mining exploitation has left indelible scars. The Australia that the elders of old knew intimately, the 'Big Body' of their ancestral spirit, has passed on into the Dreaming. Its network of tribal boundaries, languages, sacred songs, rituals and ceremonies are little more than memories for those who have managed to survive. The luminous edifice of belief which once towered over all has crumbled. What remains is a ruin, a few crumbling walls of sacred knowledge. Only now, and almost too late, are we beginning to recognize this to be one of the great achievements of the human spirit. Transforming a material landscape into a spiritual one required an act of imaginal integrity that we today have lost the capacity to emulate. In a sense we have become less human or, shall we say, less able to identify with the supra-human in the wake of this loss.

For many years now I have travelled the Australian Outback in search of origins. I have visited numerous caves, their walls daubed in strange hieroglyphs and images of Dreaming figures.

Encountering Myth

I have talked with Aboriginal elders about their history and culture, and how their people have managed to weather their traumatic encounter with the white man. I have listened to their stories, and heard their songs. I have felt my own throat contract in thrilling anticipation whilst hearing the priestly language of sacred chants emanating from the lips of tribal sages well versed in the knowledge of their totems and their Dreaming heroes. I have gazed upon sacred *churinga*, the ancient icon stones and wooden boards associated with the wanderings of ancestral heroes at the time of the Dreaming. But most of all, with the help of my Aboriginal friends, I have learnt how to listen to the voice of the land, this 'speaking land', as it whispers its entreaties. Everything I have seen and done during the course of my travels has led me closer to an understanding of how unique the earth upon which all of us walk really is — not just in Australia but throughout the world.

Because of these experiences I have learned to accept the fact that the way to a deeper knowledge of the earth involved an appreciation of mythogenesis — that is, the making of myths. Living in a country where the original inhabitants still understand this process has made it much easier for me to enter into the spirit of fashioning an imaginal landscape out of the bones of the earth. The physical sciences such as chemistry, biology and geology, for example, only give a partial view of the substance that sustains us. Yet in contrast science is unable to penetrate the deeper substratum of knowledge inherent in the earth — a knowledge that can only be explained by way of myth and metaphor. Rather than enhancing the meaning of the earth as central to our lives, the loss of mythogenic experience had left us bereft of an essential ingredient required for a true understanding of what it means to 'stem from the earth'.

It occurred to me also that perhaps it was impossible for someone from the modern world to experience mythogenesis any more. It was as if a vital human faculty, primordial in its origins, had ceased to function, just as the wings on a penguin or an emu are no longer capable of flight. Could it be that our preoccupation with logical thought, particularly in the West since the time of the late Socratic philosophers, has precipitated a corresponding stunting of the mythic mind? It was a valid question — a question that should be tested if we are to condemn mythogenesis to the ashcan of history as a relic of an earlier pattern of behaviour and thought. I needed to know, firstly, whether mythogenesis could continue to enunciate transcendent ideals over and above those of material reality, or whether it had become an exhausted or even a decadent form of expression. It seemed that inherent in the activity itself was a way of thinking which precluded material reality (i.e. the scientific process as we know it) because such a reality inhibited the entry of the mind (and by implication, the intellect) into that rarified realm where a theophany might begin to occur.

According to the philosophers, a theophanic experience is one whereby a man is able to achieve full access to the intermediate suprasensory world in which the active imagination perceives events, figures and presences in a direct form, unaided by the senses. The mythic imagination makes it possible to partake of such an experience. Entering into a myth allows the pilgrim to make an interior journey in the company of spirit identities that exist on another plane altogether. He is able to take leave of himself not only for the duration of the myth (in the context of ritual or story telling) but for his entire life, since he acknowledges the mythogenic realm as central to it anyway. Such a suprasensory encounter allows him the opportunity to experience himself as both a mortal being in the sense of his humanity, as well as an immortal being in the sense of his mythical association with spirit-entities.

I realized that if I were to begin to re-learn the language of myth, particularly as it related to a culture so ancient as that of the Australian Aborigines, it would be necessary to shrug off an accumulation of prejudices and assumptions about the nature of pre-logical thinking. I could not simply regard their mythic viewpoint as antecedent to mine. Instead I would have to learn how to participate in mythogenesis not only as a novice

12

encountering the curve of symbols for the first time, but as someone who had learnt to understand its significance after many years of thought and discussion, or through revelation by my peers. This is how the Aborigines would have participated in mythogenesis. The young *iliara* (novice) would, at some point in his education, hear a myth for the very first time. He would encounter its parade of events, its paradoxical and often non-sensical contents, knowing that at some stage in his life it was incumbent on him to comprehend its inner message. This was what I would have to do in order to open the door to that incomparable treasury of myths still awaiting an encounter with my feelings of surprise and joy. Furthermore, I would have to learn to become an *iliara*, and begin to listen to the voice of the land as it recounted its message to me.

This was not so easy as it sounded. To begin with, there is little opportunity to become initiated into a tribe these days, as the old tribal structures barely exist. Receiving scarifications to the body or losing my foreskin in a ritual act were out of the question also. Even the elders I had spoken to over the years admitted to me the fragility of these customs among their own people. Physical displacement, exile, white man's education and religious instruction — these were only some of the impediments that have made the initiation rituals of today little more than pale imitations of those that were performed in the past. Yet while the Aboriginal elders were familiar with the ways of white men, spoke English, drove cars and collected their pension cheques each month, they were also steeped in the old ways of their culture. They still lived in a mythic world. They still revered their Dreaming ancestors with an intensity that defied analysis. It became clear to me that the trauma of European contact over the past two hundred years had not shaken their faith in the Dreaming in the least. They still thought in a mythic way, enabling them to rise above the tragedy of their cultural disintegration in the wake of European settlement, so that they might live out what was left of their proud Dreaming tradition.

In place of tribal initiation there was only one alternative: to

13

take a number of myths and explore all their ramifications at the level of Aboriginal insight as well as that of the Primordial Tradition. Mythogenesis is a universal experience, after all, spanning space and time. The great myth-cycles of the Native Americans rival those of the Indian Vedas. A Dogon villager in West Africa has ordered his universe with the same due consideration as that of his Iban counterpart in the forests of Borneo. The South American Kogi Indian has built up a cosmos as complete as that of any devotee of Hathor or Isis among the ancient Egyptians. If there were parallels in these traditions, and if these parallels could be placed within the mythic context of Aboriginal culture, then there was a chance that at least some of the great myths of this benighted people might be polished to a point where they would begin to reflect a reality for me as well. In other words, I might learn to recognize myself in those ancestral spirits whose world-creating activity at the time of the Dreaming had provided Aborigines with a meaning to life.

Mythogenesis does not evolve from the imagination of men. Therefore myth-making is not a product of men's minds. It does not occur because men choose to create a story which imposes 'sense' on the world at large. This kind of thinking might be applicable to the creation of a folktale or a yarn, which may find its source in conventional reality or an historical event. The origin of myth lies elsewhere, in the intermediate world where the senses give way to a more subtle, presential knowledge emanating from the soul itself. Such a knowledge derives its effect from what may be termed 'pristine recognition' — that is, the ability to discern the contours of a celestial realm wholly given over to the enactment of so-called 'events in heaven'. These events make up the substance of myth, and can only be explained through mythogenesis. Thus we are not looking at events which occur in time, but those which transpire outside time altogether.

The challenge was to enter into a pre-logical thought mode in order to discover how extensive mythogenesis can be as a means of expressing the reality and truth of these so-called 'events in heaven'. For the Aborigines such events are clearly recognized as being those of their ancestral spirit-entities at the time of the Dreaming. The Dreaming is their Heaven, their Paradise, ndeed the repository of all their sublunary thoughts about the nature of the otherworld. It does not exist in time or place, nor does it have a physical dimension in the form of some paradisiacal garden. Nonetheless it exists as a mythogenic terrain, a place where truth is couched in a form in which they can recognize themselves. The events of the Dreaming become a projection *onto the land* of all the theophanies inherent in the activities of Creation.

Surrounding oneself within a mythic envelope is one way of obtaining an insight into the pre-logical thought process. By hearing myths related, by listening to the chants associated with their ritual enactment, by watching Aboriginal songmen and dancers setting themselves apart from this world in order to undertake a Dream journey, such methods help one to identify with the personage of the spirit-beings in their many guises. Whether they be Eaglehawk or Namanjolk, the Rainbow Serpent or Daliman Wandjina, or indeed the countless regional masks these entities choose to wear, there will always be some consistency about their adopted personas. Remote, fickle, sometimes cruel and barbaric, devoid of all human feeling or emotion, illogical in their behaviour, often incapable of trust or friendship, immune from psychological pressure and utterly resistant to the entreaties of the Aborigines themselves, these spirit-entities command a degree of respect and reverence inconceivable to someone raised on the principles of a 'just God' or the more benign ramifications of the Christian myth. Their actions transcend those of humankind in a way that generates both confusion and awe. Even their motives are devoid of psychological emphasis, reminding us that their entire spiritual persona is 'empty', a shell so to speak, pre-existent and existing in the wake of their world-creation. It is clear that they have no reason for ordering chaos at the beginning of time — at least no *earthly* reason that we can understand.

Encountering Myth

In the end we are left with a 'way of being', a glorious self-contradiction upon which to feast our thought and belief. A Dreaming hero manifests himself as a brilliant flash of intuition, a figure utterly immune from the prefigurations of gain or loss. He does not pretend to be good, nor does he glory in the idea of evil. He is simply amoral, unshackled by any dichotomy between right and wrong. Nor does he speak to us through any conceptual formularization in the way of dogma; instead he expresses himself as a vital force in everything that happens to him in the context of a myth. We are left with a kind of feathery construct, a series of Dreaming events which resist all our attempts to understand their meaning. Yet equally we are intoxicated by their bizarre majesty, their ability to get below the skin of our mind and tantalise us with suggestion and allusion. They are like night birds: we perceive their presence as an onrush of wind, but we cannot see them flying by.

We are therefore faced with a dilemma. Do we back away from the incomprehensible nature of mythogenesis, or do we accept the myth for what it is: a key, a metaphoric device, a set of remarkable images which, when embraced in the proper spirit, leads to a genuine theophanic experience? If we continue to regard myth as a relic of pre-logical thought, then we remove ourselves from the possibility of coming to terms with the earth as a glorious body imbued with certain pristine qualities. We accept it for what it is, a geomorphic reality whose origin lies in the mist of time, surrounded by concepts and categories pertaining to its physical birth as a result of some solar or inter-galactic frission. In so doing we condemn the earth to a condition of living in a state of spiritual inertness, a state which Aborigines cannot contemplate without a feeling of abhorrence.

On the other hand, if we decide to embark upon a journey into the earth as a mythic excursion, then we must equip ourselves with an entirely different set of categories. We cannot look at the earth as physical representation. We cannot view it either in terms of economics, agriculture, industry or indeed as the basis for leisure. We must completely divorce ourselves from the perception of the earth as a passive value wholly controlled by ourselves. To mine it or to farm it, to transform it into a tourist environment, or to re-arrange it in conformity with practical values immediately separates us from its intrinsic otherness. This is why Aborigines never attempted to alter their tribal landscape. They saw it as complete, utterly realized in terms of its principial virtues. Thus to mine a hill or valley sacred to certain Dreaming heroes is to tamper with the very substance of their belief. Once the spirit of the land has been abused in any way, it becomes impossible to regard that place as any more a repository of *kurunba* or 'earth wisdom'. It becomes instead what Aborigines refer to as 'rubbish country'.

Such thoughts made it clear that I must embrace the mythic experience without any pre-conditions. I had to allow myself to be taken in by mythic events in a way that they might evoke a state of mind whereby I could see the earth in a wholly different light. In a sense, I would have to allow mythogenesis to impose its conditions on me! The scholar, the poet, even the thinker in me had to be put aside in the interest of realizing a new set of prerogatives, those relating to earth knowledge. I had to accept that how I might view the world in the context of my own upbringing was not at all in conformity with the way a pre-logical thinker like the Aborigine might view it. His education had given him a set of subjective values completely different from mine. As a result, he was able to perceive certain verities which were no longer visible to me, except in terms of a vague racial memory that I still believed I possessed. But I could not rely on such a memory as it had no basis in any system of thought with which I was familiar. Like the blind, limbless man often portrayed in early Aboriginal creation-myths, I was to find myself devoid of any power of gesture except that of mere presence. As yet I had no right to call myself a fully initiated man into the mysteries of earth knowledge until I had embraced fully the mythogenic experience.

Before me, then, lay the task of unravelling myths. Not only must I set foot on the landscape of myth, but I also had to learn how to take the myth apart piece by piece and re-assemble it again. Only by going through this process would it be possible to understand what was occurring in the mind of a songman as he chanted his sacred songs. Furthermore, if I were going to be able to walk across the earth of Australia as a true 'man of knowledge' in the future, I would have to begin to think in a different way. I would have to accept the Dreaming heroes of the Aborigines as part of my own spiritual pantheon.

Of course there are literarily thousands of myths to choose from. The Red Centre alone abounds in Dreaming trails. These record the movement of the spirit-beings across the landscape, their imposition of form in the way of every hill, gully, stream and cave, and their dissemination of sacred law for humankind to live by after their dematerialization. No place on the map has escaped their originatory gesture in the form of mythic explanation. These places have all been named, and they perpetuate an existence that is entirely otherworldy. Language has embraced their immutable forms and transformed these into a topography of prose and ritual. No place is silent in the wake of the passage of these spirit-beings at the time of the Dreaming. Every corner of the earth is blessed with its own story, its own narrative desire to enter the minds of men as a sequence of divine events. It is enough for Aborigines to translate the language of the land into meaningful data which enables them to fulfil their role as an extension to these events.

In the first part of this book I have chosen to investigate a myth which deals with world-creation, with the appearance of human exemplars, and with the delineation of natural law as it relates to the people who make Central Australia their home. The myth dealt with explores a celestial encounter with the earth in the form of a Dreaming hero's exploits, and how Aborigines integrate these exploits culturally. Initially the material will be presented in its raw form — that is, as it has been recorded by various field workers. Clearly how this material is interpreted by both informant and researcher is important to the overall unravelling of the myths; but as important is the way the material evokes significant echoes in traditions from other parts of the world. It is only by linking the Aboriginal myth with its archetype elsewhere (in place and in time) that we can recognize its universality, and so regard it as a part of the combined opus of human spirituality and thought. By seeking to emphasise similarities rather than differences, it is hoped that the full splendour of the Aboriginal mythic repertoire will be revealed.

In the second part of the book a series of creation-myths and their associated songs and rituals from the northern part of Australia, in the region known as Arnhem Land will be investigated. These myths deal with the Kunapipi or Great Mother rituals, their link with the myth of the Wauwalak Sisters and their encounter with Julungul, the Rainbow Snake.

In the third part of the book certain Wandjina myth-cycles from the Kimberley region of north-west Australia are explored, a region markedly different from elsewhere in Australia in the way the Dreaming heroes chose to manifest themselves in the form of cloud-men. Stylistically, all three regions incorporate symbolic motifs and a visual iconography which emphasize this difference. In the north we encounter the 'X-ray' style of rock art; in the northwest the 'cloud-image' style; while in the Red Centre 'dot and circle' iconography prevails. Although each art-style appears to imply a significant contrast in the respective mythic traditions, it will be seen that in spite of vast climatic and territorial differences (Arnhem Land and the Kimberley are subject to monsoonal activity each year, while Central Australia is an extremely arid landscape), the underlying metaphysic of the peoples living in these regions remains essentially the same.

Ultimately the Dreaming is a metaphysical condition which prevails over all. The Great Snake meanders along all the major watercourses, his serpentine body an affront to the idea of chaos. The mountain ranges, the bluffs, the still valleys and the plains find their present form in the activities of individual spirit-beings. Every cave, tree, waterhole, every bird, animal and insect owes its existence to a Dreaming event of sorts. Aboriginal man himself is not a self-creation, but a manifestation of a reincarnated spirit from the Dreaming. He sees himself as not born into this world for the first time, but as someone who carries within him an otherworldly legacy which his spirit is required to transmit to each new generation from time immemorial. During the course of these pages we will meet with men who have 'lived before', with men who carry the wound of the first man inside their bodies, with men who have possessed mythogenic knowledge since the time of their conception in a dream. Furthermore we will be encountering a race of men who acknowledge themselves to be not representatives of 'fallen man' so to speak, but rather believe themselves to be heralds or emissaries of their Dreaming heroes.

The mythic journey is one that we all must dare to take if we are to begin to embrace our own origins in a genuine spirit of renewal. Our love-affair with the material condition has turned us outward, away from the great free spaces of the imagination wherein the wandering soul is entertained by those nomads of the spirit. The latter, of course, are invisible; they inhabit only that region of the mind which we refuse to constrain. Like an unbridled horse, the myth is capable of transporting us into this region as a freely moving vitality, a spiritual energy which will not be reined in to suit any logical imperative that we might seek to impose. It is up to all of us to mount and be unafraid as we ride forward into that numinous terrain sacred to the Dreaming heroes. That is, if we wish to re-discover the ancient *churinga* with its whorls and lines, denoting none other than our contiguity with the spirit of the earth.

CHAPTER 2
In the Footsteps of Ankotarinja

North of the blue ridged MacDonnell Ranges (Pota Tjoritja), not far from the road between Alice Springs and the Tanami Desert, lies a shallow watercourse near a totem centre known as Ankota. It is not a particularly memorable place in terms of its physical features, lying as it does on a scrubby plain within the vicinity of Mt. Solitaire. But Ankota's mythical presence makes it an extremely significant spiritual centre — as significant for the Aranda people, perhaps, as Jerusalem or Mecca are to Christians and Moslems. For Ankota is the birthplace of Ankotarinja, the Dreaming hero who first emerged from the ground to create the world.

Ankotarinja, the first man, is both a primal man and a wild dog (dingo). His myth belongs, or belonged (since the last tribal custodian died in Alice Springs many years ago) to a small band of Aranda men who once lived in the vicinity of Ankota, known as the Ngala-Mbitjana people.[1] They were heirs to Ankotarinja's exploits at the time of the Dreaming, performing his ceremonies, initiating their young *iliara* into his totemic lodge, and keeping alive the memory of his world-creating endeavours from one generation to the next. No one knows when Ankotarinja first emerged from the creekbed near Ankota, but according to the Aborigines today his manifestation on earth happened 'long-time ago'. Which means that Ankotarinja, the dingo-man of Ankota, had been a part of ancestral memory for as long as anyone can remember.

T.G.H. Strehlow, a Lutheran pastor's son from Hermansburg Mission in Central Australia, was the first man to record the myth of Ankotarinja. He also happened to speak fluent Aranda, the result of playing with Aranda children around the mission during the years of his youth. A sensitive and sympathetic observer of Aboriginal custom and belief during his own lifetime, Strehlow sought to defend Aborigines all his life. He

21

was a man with 'inside knowledge', since he had been granted his own totemic country near the Hermansburg Mission by an Aboriginal elder who accepted him (Strehlow) as its custodial heir before his own death. Subsequently that country belonged to Strehlow, along with its songs, its ceremonies and the secret information known only to his custodial brothers.

Strehlow was critical of what he called the 'primitivist' school of anthropologists at work in his day. He saw them as being too willing to over-emphasize the difference between Aborigines and ourselves, a situation that he felt stemmed from the language barrier that existed between most anthropologists and their informants. 'Too often traditions and customs were noted down in their barest outlines,' he once wrote, 'and the details later filled in by the scientists themselves according to their conception of what the natives' ideas *ought* to have been on certain subjects.'[2] Inevitably such interpretations cast Aborigines in the mould of being little more than a highly specialized offshoot of the human species, 'primitive and incapable of further development', and therefore doomed to extinction. In contrast, Strehlow believed that Aboriginal legends and chants represented a living memorial to the origin of all poetry. It was a true hieratic language.

The Ankotarinja myth had been passed on to him by an old man before he died in Alice Springs in 1932. The man had been the last reincarnation of Ankotarinja, and so embodied the spirit of the Dreaming hero not only in his physical being, but also in the form of the sacred *churinga* stones associated with the totemic centres located along the Dreaming trail of the spirit-being. According to Strehlow, these *churinga* and the man who told him the Ankotarinja myth, were 'one body' — that they formed the 'supernatural deathless body' of the Dreaming hero himself. How a man and Dreaming hero like Ankotarinja could be linked to so many *churinga*, and also constitute 'one body', Strehlow tried to explain by making a comparison between the different phases of the moon. 'Each night, between the dates of the first quarter and the last moon, offers a slightly different picture to the observer,' he noted. 'Yet all these different "moons" are one and the same heavenly body. In the same way, the different *churinga* depict Ankotarinja at different stages or "phases" of his life. Nonetheless they are *all* the one body of this man. Taken together they form the one body which has undergone all these varied experiences.' Like the wine and wafer of Christian liturgy, the sacred *churinga* embodied the spirit of Ankotarinja just as the former embodied the spirit of Jesus Christ.

Churinga are much more than inscribed stones or boards. They represent the timeless presence of the Dreaming hero here on earth.[3] Usually wrapped in dry leaves, bound with string made from human hair and kept either on a platform or in a crevasse near the totemic centre, *churinga* are, in a sense, the collective numen of the spirit-being, his *kurunba*. They must be treated with the same respect and reverence as one might treat the secret information of the myth itself. As one informant advised his son, 'This is your own body from which you have been reborn. This is the true body of the great Tjenterama, the chief of the Ilbalintja storehouse. You are the great Tjenterama himself: today you are learning the truth for the first time. From now on all the sacred *churinga* are entrusted to your safekeeping. Protect them and guard the home of your fathers, honour the traditions of your people.'[4] In this way, both the tradition and the metaphysical absence of the Dreaming hero are made present in the *churinga*. They represent an Aborigine's link with the otherworld.

Before recounting the myth of Ankotarinja, it is important that we gain at least a residual idea of how the Dreaming hero manifests himself in a mythic sense. Of course he has no material form as such. We may picture him, therefore, in the way as do those Aborigines nominated to perform the rituals linked to his world-birth, since these man have been informed of the dog-man's Dreaming-image by the elders before them. Like the Turin Shroud, or the image of Christ as depicted by the monk painters on Mt. Athos in Greece, there is a sacred 'image' of

23

Ankotarinja which has been passed down through the ages. This image is said to have been revealed by the Dreaming hero himself.

We must try to visualize Ankotarinja not simply as a dingo, a canine which walks about on all fours. Nor should we see him as an ordinary man. He is much more than both. At the moment of his world-birth the performers see him in terms of his sacred body-paintings (which never vary) and the presence of the Dreaming hero's *churinga* in their headgear. We may say that Ankotarinja 'looks like' a man, a dingo, an abstract body-painting, a head-dress featuring sacred *churinga* boards, and an invisible presence — all at the same time. Since he is a genuine spirit-being, we must try to see him also as a divine abstraction which nonetheless embodies the relentless will and shiftlessness of a wild dog, the active and audacious masculinity of a man and the invisible *pneuma* of a spirit. His form may also take on the strange feeling of silence that one encounters when approaching his sacred birthplace near Ankota. The very nervousness one feels is a part of his manifestation, since it partakes of what Walter Otto called the 'intimate and dear, the seductive and frightening' ambience that one find in the vicinity of sacred places.[5]

Here then is an imaginal portrait of Ankotarinja, the dog-man of Ankota, the Dreaming hero who emerged from the earth in a dry creekbed for the first time. He lives on as the incarnation of a 'momentary god' — that is, as an intensification of our sense experience to the point where we believe we have his image within our grasp. As Meister Eckhart wrote of God, so too may Ankotarinja be likened to 'the simple ground, the still desert, the simple silence'. In the very act of naming him, Ankotarinja becomes someone existent and significant in his own right. A spark has ignited the tinder of his mythogenesis, releasing an inner excitement which was merely a vague subjective state in us prior to this moment. From now on he becomes the objective form of a myth as depicted in language and ritual. Ankotarinja becomes the ancestral hero of the Ngala-Mbitjana band who

once lived near his birthplace.
The myth begins:

In the beginning, there is a man living at Ankota who has
emerged from the earth without father or mother. Before this
moment, he has been lying asleep in the depths of the earth where
white ants have eaten his body to the bone. The soil rests on him like
a blanket. While he is lying there, he thinks: "Perhaps it might be
nice to rise up and stand." He lies there, pondering what he should
do. Finally he arises from the soft soil of the creekbed for the first
time.

Still half asleep, he looks around. He sees a host of great
tnatantjas or ceremonial poles standing in the sand. These *tnatantjas*
belong to other men and women who have emerged from the earth
in the same way that he has. For a moment he hesitates, wondering
what to do next. He stands on legs that are still weak and tottering.
His body is like a skeleton where the white ants have been feeding
on him. He stands there listlessly, uncertain of his next move.

Then Ankotarinja staggers to the edge of a nearby swamp and
sits down. He gazes at himself as he reflects on his new-born
condition. What he sees as he begins to decorate his body with red
down is a great *tnatantja* rearing up from the crown of his head. It
has been there ever since he first emerged from the ground. And
when he looks at his own image in the water, Ankotarinja sees that
the ceremonial pole sprouting from his head reaches so high it
touches the dome of the sky.

Ankotarinja begins to breathe heavily, like a dingo, as he sniffs
the four winds. He feels a cold breeze blowing from the north. A
cold breeze is blowing also from the south and east. But when he
turns to the west he feels a warm breeze on his face. He draws the
warmth to him and cries out, "The breeze that warms my heart
comes from the west!" As he speaks, the great tnatantja towering
above his head topples to the ground. He climbs to his feet then and
sets out on his journey westward, towards the source of the warm
breeze.

But rather than travel overland Ankotarinja decides to journey
underneath the ground. At a place called Irbunngurerea (about
seventy miles west of Ankota), on the other side of Tnira, he
emerges once again. There he notices footprints on the ground
belonging to a band of unknown women. He notices also where
they have been digging for frogs in a creekbed. He remarks to
himself, "There is no fire burning here, so where have they gone?"

In the Footsteps of Ankotarinja

He crouches low, stretches himself like a dog, then continues to trail their scent.

At last he spies burning coals at a camp in another location. "They must have left here a short while before," he says to himself eagerly.

Crouching still lower he hurries forward until he sees the women's figures in the distance, sitting crosslegged, eating. The women, meanwhile, suddenly begin to feel ill. "Who has made us feel so sick?" they ask one another. Helplessly they sit there, unable to eat or move, gazing into the distance. Ankotarinja, however, has cleverly concealed himself from their gaze.

While they are gazing into the distance with their eyes raised, looking for the source of their illness, Ankotarinja sneaks up on them, crouching low in the grass. He is able to draw close to them and prepare his attack. Without warning, he leaps from the grass and sinks his fangs into the waists of two women before they can escape. He crushes them between his teeth, then moves on to his real quarry which he spies from the crest of a hill.

Below, Ankotarinja, the dog-man, sees the home of the *tilpa* men of Parr Erultja. He watches them closely to ascertain their behaviour. He remains utterly still, hardly breathing, like a dingo ready to pounce. Then he slowly inches forward, all the while taking in the *tilpa* men with his gaze. Unwittingly the ;tilpa8 men are lying stretched out on the ground at the foot of their great ceremonial *tnatantja*, sleeping soundly. These too are reaching forth into the sky, touching the blue dome above.

Ankotarinja pounces on his quarry. He attacks one man after another. Like a whirlwind he rakes them all together, snatching at them fiercely. As he kills them, so too does he eat them all one by one. Unable to eat another *tilpa* man now that his stomach is so full, Ankotarinja grows sleepy and stretches himself out at the foot of the *tnatantja* for a nap.

Meanwhile another man journeys from farther west towards Parr Erultja in the east. Arriving at Parr Erultja, he notices that no one is around. "Where are all the *tilpa* men?" he asks himself. "They seems to have all gone, and the wind that used to blow from here no longer does, either." Then he notices Ankotarinja lying at the foot of the *tnatantja*, gorged and half asleep.

The man from the west approaches the *tilpa* camp cautiously. He looks down from the crest of a low hill, and sees an object lying at the foot of the *tnatantja*. What he sees however is not a man but a monster, blind and lacking eyes, gleaming red in the firelight. The man from the west approaches on all fours, his anger kindled. He wants to avenge the deaths of the *tilpa* men.

When he draws closer to the monster he spits on his hands. Then he hurls a sacred *churinga* at the monster, hitting him in the nape of the neck. Ankotarinja's head rolls away, making it possible for the swallowed *tilpa* men to be disgorged. They flow forth from the trunk of the monster like water. At once they climb up on the rocky hills around Parr Erultja, shouting with joy and swinging their bullroarers merrily. To celebrate their rebirth they decorate their heads with green twigs and wallaby tails.

Meanwhile the monster's dead body lies inert on the ground, although his severed head is still alive. Ankotarinja's head reflects, "My home isn't so far away, really. Let me go back there for my last rest." So his head rolls back towards Ankota underneath the ground, to emerge finally in the creekbed where he was born. There it passes into the earth again and remains forever.[6]

The myth of Ankotarinja ends where it began — in the dry creekbed where the first man emerged from the earth. His head, the 'monstrous head', re-enters the world-womb just as the *tilpa* men entered his mouth and stomach at Parr Erultja at the foot of the great *tnatantja*, that world-tree and *axis mundi*. It is hard to imagine a simpler story than this one. A Dreaming hero is born, contemplates himself, goes on an underground journey, attacks and consumes women, then men, falls asleep and is attacked by another, a foreigner from the west, before being decapitated and later returning to his place of origin. In this tale we find echoes of mythic heroes from many regions and cultures of the world. Gilgamesh, Heracles, the Green Knight, the legendary Round Table knights, Indra and Namuci, Osiris — these are but some of the heroes which populate myths ranging from Sumeria, Greece, Celtic Europe, India and Egypt. That Ankotarinja does not wear greaves, carry a sword, or bedeck himself in robes in no way inhibits his legendary status. After all, his every action implies his mythic entity, since none of them strike us in any way as being inspired by normal human motives. The world he enters as a momentary god is transformed forever by his movements. Ankota and Parr Erultja have become sacred centres; the eternal tension between divine entity and men has been heralded in the form of the *tilpa* men's consumption, followed by the man from the west's revenge; and we are confronted with the 'resolution of the head' — that is, the divine intellect's return to its primordial birthplace at the centre of the world, minus its material body. The apotheosis of Oedipus, Buddha and Christ finds their echo in Ankotarinja's dematerialization and his descension ('to climb down') into primordial matter. Though he is lost to us in the physical sense he never really dies, otherwise there could not exist any life-giving *churinga* of him for men to share.

But these did and do exist. According to Strehlow, who saw Ankotarinja's stone *churinga* at Ankota when he was taken there by his informant, the old man from Alice Springs — Ankotarinja's most recent reincarnation. Two very old stone *churinga* located in the storehouse at Ankota represented the Dreaming hero's life, his *kurunba* or quickening power. On the other hand, four wooden *churinga* representing his deathless other body remained at Parr Erultja, so signifying Ankotarinja's presence there (minus his head). The old man from Alice Springs, whose secret name was Ankotarinja (Aborigines often possess a public and a secret name), regarded the two stone *churinga* as his own body, while acknowledging also that the four wooden ones from Parr Erultja were a part of this same supernatural body in which he participated. It is clear that Ankotarinja still 'lived' not only in his human reincarnation, but in the various stone and wooden *churinga* as well. It follows that Strehlow had met and received the myth from the Dreaming hero himself. Both the man and the *churinga* embodied Ankotarinja in a formal unity that can only be described as being of significant mystical import.

These points need to be emphasized so that there is no confusion about what we are dealing with here. World-ordering by mythic heroes establish criteria by which men subsequently live. They in turn enact the Dreaming hero's birth and journey. They sing the songs denoting individual events. They take on the persona of the spirit-being when they daub themselves in eagle

28

down and pipeclay. Every element of the myth is drawn into the participants by these acts of mimesis. At the same time, the isolated occurrence of the myth and its separation from the totality of ordinary, commonplace experience produces not only a tremendous intensification, but also the highest degree of *condensation*, so that the objective form of the Dreaming hero seems to burst forth from the experience itself. The listener and/or participants find themselves captivated and enthralled by the intuition that suddenly confronts them in the form of the Dreaming hero's actions. These actions are not logical in any way, and so are capable of breaking down any illusion of intellectual unity that might have existed prior to that moment.

The various *churinga* mentioned earlier, each of which has a different name that is reflected in the ceremonial verses themselves, act as 'word icons'. The verses are known as *churinga retnja* which means 'names of the *churinga*'. This means that the *churinga* are both scintillas of the spirit-being and representations of his 'word'. All this implies a precedence of language over the outward form and manifestation of the myth. In the highest sense mythology is the power exercised by language on thought in every possible sphere of mental activity.[7] In the case of the Ankotarinja myth we are confronted with a series of eighteen verses which describe the actions of the dog-man. Of these, the first five verses describe Ankotarinja at rest in his burrow. They in turn are linked to the principal stone *churinga* located at Ankota. On the other hand, when one of the wooden *churinga* from Parr Erultja is being shown, this is at once linked to the final chant in the song. If this happens, then the chant is likely to consist of a series of such word-icons or 'names' of individual *churinga* strung together. The *churinga* become an adjunct to the myth or, more precisely, they embody the myth.

Which leaves us poised in the presence of the songmen who actually enact the myth in their ceremonies. These men are custodians of the songs; they belong to them as an inherited possession, and cannot be sung by any other except where the owner's permission has been granted. Furthermore, these chants are all carefully graded in rising degrees of secrecy and sacredness. They can only be revealed to men who have shown themselves fit to receive the secret-sacred information. It is interesting to note in this respect that there are more often than not two versions of a myth — a correct, secret one and a false, public version. In the case of the Ankotarinja myth the false version recounts an overland journey to Parr Erultja, not an underground one. The traditional custodians ridicule the false version while at the same time condoning its existence. In a sense, the false version 'deflects' inquiry away from the true, esoteric version of the myth. Moreover knowledge of the true version enhances the status of the traditional custodians. They are in possession of information that only a select elite are entitled to know. This includes the body-painting designs, the dance rituals and the decorative patterns that may be painted on the *inkura* or sacred ceremonial ground. Of all the objects that Aborigines own their myth material constitutes their most prized possession. It has been given to them to hold in trust by the Dreaming heroes themselves.

The chants bring us in contact with the full numinosity of the myth itself. Not only is the language used hieratic in tone, but it deliberately sets out to distort and sometimes dismember everyday speech. Speech accent gives way to verse accent, while the vowels undergo a change both in quantity and quality when united to the rhythm of the verse. The language of mythogenesis is truly transformative, designed to act as a bridge for participants and audience alike so that they might cross over into the rarified realm wherein divine events are played out.

Here then is a translation of the Ankotarinja chants, depicting the birth of the dog-man, his journey to Parr Erultja, His attack on the *tilpa* men, and his eventual return to Ankota, together with a brief description of the events described:[8]

Verses one to five describe Ankotarinja in his burrow at Ankota 'at the beginning of time'. He is decorated with red down, a symbol of blood and life. This is the moment of world-birth:

30

In the Footsteps of Ankotarinja

Red is the down which is covering me;
Red am I as if I were burning in fire.

Red am I as if I were burning in fire,
Red, too, is the hollow in which I am lying.

The red *churinga* is resting upon my head,
Red, too, is the hollow in which I am lying.

Red am I like the heart of a flame of fire,
Red, too, is the hollow in which I am lying.

The red *churinga* is resting on my head,
Red, too, is the hollow in which I am lying.

At the commencement of verse six we are introduced to the great *tnatantja* as it rises up into the sky:

Like a whirlwind, it is towering into the sky,
Like a pillar of red sand, it is towering into the sky.

The *tnatantja* is towering into the sky,
Like a pillar of red sand, it is towering into the sky.

Verses eight and nine describe the region around Ankota, indicating it to be desert country:

A mass of red pebbles covers the plains,
Little white sand ridges cover the plains.

Lines of red pebbles streak the plains,
Lines of white sand ridges streak the plains.

Catching the scent of the women, Ankotarinja finds an underground pathway opening before him in verses ten and eleven:

An underground pathway lies open before me,

In the Footsteps of Ankotarinja

Leading directly to the west, it lies open before me.

A cavernous pathway lies open before me,
Leading directly to the west, it lies open before me.

Ankotarinja then follows up the scent of the women in verses twelve and thirteen:

He is sucking his beard into his mouth in anger,
Like a dog he follows the trail by scent.

He hurries on swiftly, like a keen dog;
Like a dog he follows the trail by scent.

Ankotarinja attacks the *tilpa* men at Parr Erultja and eats them:

Irresistible and foaming with rage —
Like a whirlwind, he rakes them together.

After being struck down by the man from the west, Ankotarinja dreams of his home at Ankota, and decides to return by the underground pathway:

Out there, not far from me, lies Ankota;
The underground hole is gaping open before me.

A straight track is gaping open before me,
An underground hole is gaping open before me.

A cavernous pathway is gaping open before me,
An underground pathway is gaping open before me.

In the final verse Ankotarinja finds himself once more in his old homeland:

Red am I, like the heart of a flame of fire,
Red, too, is the hollow in which I am resting.

In the Footsteps of Ankotarinja

In these ageless verses which have sprung from the earth of
Central Australia, the myth of Ankotarinja unfolds. We are now
in possession of a story, a series of sacred chants, a ritual number
of body-paintings and certain knowledge pertaining to those
stone and wooden *churinga* whose *kurunba* (numen) links them
with the Dreaming hero and his activities. We are also in
possession of a series of primordial images: a birth, a skeletal
body, a world-tree, a mirror, a subterranean journey, a cannibal
act, a monster, a decapitation and a return. All these combine
to give us the precious ingredients of mythic enactment. On the
one hand we have the narrative; on the other the paraphernalia
of ritual, and all the accoutrements needed for a re-creation of
the original moment when the process of mythogenesis began.
Furthermore it means that we have journeyed to a point in time
when language is prefigured, when the first Aborigine began to
draw a magic circle around himself using ritual word-images —
a circle as if inscribed by the subtle tip of his tongue which both
freed and ensnared him. He has become a victim of the power
of the universe to enthral, to carry him out of himself. He has
become identified with the invisible forces of chaos which we
know exist, but which we cannot comprehend. How will we
know whether we, along with Ankotarinja, have quit the realm
of *consciousness* and finally entered the land beyond? One thing
is certain: there are no certainties in the process of mythogenesis.
Following in the footsteps of Ankotarinja as he descends into the
underworld may grant us a view of the legendary valley at Parr
Erultja. Then again, it may lead us down to hell.

What we do know is that many incarnations of Ankotarinja
have preceded us. He has lived before. The old man that
Strehlow knew in Alice Springs was but the last in a long line of
avataric figures. Ankotarinja may not be walking this earth right
now, but this does not mean he will not re-appear some time in
the future. The great tradition of the dog-man and his encounter
with the man from the west continues to lie dormant in the
earth, waiting to be reborn again. He sleeps as he has always
done under the earth at Ankota. In spite of the desert floods

which periodically swamp this region, as a momentary god he cannot be drowned. He remains under the 'speaking earth', awaiting his cue to rise up out of the ground again as a voice, a dance, a sacred possession, a magical stone linked to his own divine name.

CHAPTER 3
Out of the World-womb

The initial impression after hearing the myth of
Ankotarinja and listening to the songs is one of confusion. The
arbitrary nature of Ankotarinja's actions strikes us as
impenetrable, whereas the poetry of the songs suggests a
sensibility entirely at odds with the Dreaming hero's persona.
Moreover the crucible of fire which has forced him to emerge
from the earth seems suffocating, an act of cruelty similar to that
of Medieval witch-burnings. In no way do we feel we are present
at the birth of a Dreaming hero, a momentary god. Nor do we
feel that we are about to share in any transformative experience.
Yet if we look more closely at the symbolism, we find ourselves
drawn in by the power of the imagery. Fire, earth, air and water
intermingle in this first act of mythogenesis, it seems.

In the early songs Ankotarinja sees himself as though 'burning
in a fire'. He becomes the elementary fire or 'divine fire' which
is said to define the nature of the god, Mercurius. He is also the
invisible fire working in secret, the universal and scintillating
fire of the light of nature. This mercurial fire is found in the
centre of the earth, the dragon's belly, and can encompass the
revelatory light of nature and also hell-fire, the energic principle
of evil. Ankotarinja embodies the re-arrangement of the heavenly,
Dreaming powers in the lower world of matter. He, like
Mercurius, is himself of a fiery nature and remains unchanged
by it. As one alchemical text remarks, 'For it is he who overcomes
the fire, and is himself not overcome by the fire, but rests in it
as a friend, rejoicing in it'.[1] Ankotarinja rests in his 'hollow of
fire', immune from its flames, at one with its celestial heat.

At once we are alerted to Ankotarinja's real nature. He is the
power of nature forced to materialize itself. The 'hollow' where
he lies is none other than the dark, maternal cavern of life.
Hence the Hindu fire-bringer is called Matarisvan, 'he who

swells in the mother' just as Ankotarinja sees himself 'red... like the heart of a flame of fire/ Red, too, is the hollow in which I am lying'. The hollow is not only the womb, but it is also linked to the cave and stable as birthplaces of the avatar. Christ and Krishna were born in such environments. In this hollow he curls up like a dog and, paradoxically, like a snake, which, according to Philo, is the most spiritual of all creatures, a fiery nature both swift and terrible. His serpentine nature is toxic and prophylactic, qually a symbol of the good and bad daemon. Ankotarinja's persona embodies the impervious nature of Mercurius, linking the spiritual nature with the earthly, and is born into the world from the same subterranean source as later avatars. He becomes the pure act of the unconscious realizing itself.

His avataric origin is further enhanced when we return to the myth. We find there that he was born 'without father or mother'. He has no cause but himself save the magical force of his name. As stated in the *Egyptian Book of the Dead* in relation to the birth of the sun-god Ra, 'There was for him no mother who made his name for him, nor father who uttered it, saying, "I have begotten him".' Instead Ra is his own creator in that he gives himself his names — that is, his characters and powers. From this original power of speech which dwells in the demiurge arises everything else that has existence and definite being. When he speaks, he causes the birth of Dreaming heroes and men. We know that Ankotarinja 'thought' himself into being as he was the first to suggest the idea of arising from the creekbed at the dawn of time.

Which leads us to another of his guises. We know later that he makes his underground journey to the west. We also know that before he attained to form as a living skeleton, he is described as a thought or 'head'. According to Gnostic texts, the 'Head is the first emanation of the Abyss which leads to the "subdivision of the One"' and is recognized to be the sacrificial act of creation — a self-sacrificial act in this case in that Ankotarinja lends himself to this division also. The Rg Veda confirms Ankotarinja's identity as the 'Head of being' in his fiery form when it states, 'At night Agni (fire) is the Head of being, thence in the morning it is born as the rising sun'.[2] So now we begin to realize that Ankotarinja is also a personification of the sun in that he finds his origin in the fiery nature of earth, just before sunrise. This is confirmed when we discover how he travels overland to Parr Erultja in the west (i.e. following the course of the sun). More importantly, we find that he travels underground, and so turns 'right' instead of 'left' if we consider the point in front of the opening in the ground as a principial fork in the road. To go down into the earth is to follow the reverse course of the sun, though in reality it means much more. According to the Satapatha Brahmana (III. 2. I. 13), this is the path sacred to the 'Fathers', while the path to the left is the 'human' way. It further states, 'He who makes a right turn, thereby he turns yonder Sun to the right, and accordingly yonder Sun moves round these worlds from left to right (SB VII. 5. 1. 37). In other words, the sun travels from left to right on its axis throughout the night or 'underground'. We know, for example, that the mouth of the Egyptian sky goddess, Nut, 'is the Western Horizon, her vulva the Eastern Horizon through whose body the sun travels at night.' The notion of a single principle in the form of Ankotarinja facing in two opposing directions places him on the threshold of the gate of two worlds, the light and the dark. This is the opening to the underworld.

Very early in the piece we are confronted with the idea of Ankotarinja as transforming himself from an earthly entity into a solar hero. Still only half asleep at the moment of his birth (a sign of his earthiness, his unconscious state), he sees a number of *tnatantjas* towering above him, brushing against the sky. As it has been already stated these ceremonial poles signify the *axis mundi*, the Cosmic Tree. This is always located at the centre of the World. Furthermore the possibility of transcending this World is at once intimated by the *tnatantjas* brushing against the sky, the celestial condition. They represent both the upward movement of the spirit and the plenary condition of the World's beginning, the perfection of the 'first instant' before anything had been defiled, since the World had just been born. For Ankotarinja, the *tnatantjas* represent not only the place of world-birth below, but also a prefigurement of a transcendent condition which he has yet to attain. At this moment he is little more than a skeletal observer, tottering, barely able to walk, let alone able to see things n a way that is contingent with spiritual perception. He is, so to speak, 'not all there', since the myth states that he is little more than a skeleton eaten clean by white ants.

The *tnatantjas* also signify the separation of the earth and sky, the glorious partition of the watery principle of femininity from the maleness of the earth. Wallace Budge[3] suggests that this separation was necessary in order to find a path for the sun to travel, all of which accords with Ankotarinja's westward journey later on. It also suggests the birth of time and space, those principial abstractions that impose on us the notion of limitation. The presence of the *tnatantjas* standing before Ankotarinja provides us with the concept of *dimension*, that the Dreaming hero has indeed entered the world as we know it. They are representations of the legendary beanstalk which Jack climbs to his rendezvous with the giant. They are the celestial cord that Aboriginal *mekigars* or clever-men are said to climb when they wish to converse with Dreaming heroes, or to travel across country. In every way these *tnatantjas* signify the radiant possibilities inherent in world-birth, partition and the mysterious dualities represented by earth and water, male and female.

This in itself confirms the link between Ankotarinja and the Cosmic Tree. At the moment of his birth he is compared to a skeleton, a 'trunk' who has provided white ants with their nourishment. White ants, after all, are not flesh-eaters but wood-eaters. Ankotarinja in his earthly condition prior to world-birth was little more than an ant-riddled trunk incapable of standing up like a tall tree, like the *tnatantjas* which graced the sky. His weakness is symptomatic of his pre-conscious condition as a celestial being, as a Dreaming hero able to chart the course of the sun at a later stage in his development. All he can do is totter about and gaze at his alter ego in the form of these *tnatantjas*

38

brushing against the sky. For they are embodiments of himself as Dreaming hero, not as a pre-existent chthonic being. As yet he is not able to partake of their reality as celestial trees.

When Ankotarinja goes to the edge of the swamp and sits down to think, we begin to see a transition from his condition as an earthly being. He becomes an embodiment of Narcissus, the boy-figure who fell in love with his own reflection in the water. Ankotarinja gazes at himself. He begins to decorate himself with red down, a symbol of blood and life. It is the mysterious rose-coloured blood that flows forth from the side of the 'Son of the Great World' and represents the quintessential essence of the Dreaming hero and nature, with its power to quicken all things. Ankotarinja 'comes to life' as a conscious, thinking being, someone who becomes aware of himself. The 'tottering skeleton' of the past has been replaced by a Dreaming hero in touch with his interior self, even if he is not yet ready to integrate that self with the world in general. He is still an introverted being. At the same time he becomes aware of a great *tnatantja* extending from his head as it reaches towards the sky.

This is a moment of supreme importance for Ankotarinja. He is made conscious of the fact that what rises from his head is a Philosophic Tree, and that it has been on his head from the very moment of his emergence from the earth, from his inception. He has been carrying his destiny on the crown of his head without perceiving it. According to Gerard Dorn, a seventeenth-century alchemist, the fruit of this tree 'strives up to heaven' where it makes contact with the 'living things of nature'.[4] Ankotarinja, in his narcissistic state, is yet able to observe aspects of his own being beyond that of his reflection. The tree is a symbol of self.

The presence of this *tnatantja* further links him to the idea of an inverted tree. The Renaissance humanist Andrea Alciati says in his *Emblemata cum commentariis* 'man is a tree standing upside down, for what in the one is the root, trunk and leaves, in the other is the head and the rest of the body'. Krishna says in the Bhagavad Gita (ch.15) 'I am the Himalayas among mountains and the *ashvatattha* among trees'. The Bhagavad Gita goes on to describe the *ashvatattha* as:

> The everlasting,
> Rooted in heaven,
> Its branches earthward;
> Each of its leaves
> Is the song of the Vedas,
> And he knows it
> Knows the vedas.
>
> Downwards and upwards
> Its branches bending
> Are fed by the gunas,
> The buds it puts forth
> Are the things of the senses,
> Roots it has also
> Reaching downward
> Into this world,
> The roots of man's action.[5]

Hindu literature places the tree firmly in the context of divine knowledge, a living process as well as a process of enlightenment which, though it may be grasped by the intellect, should not be confused with it. Ankotarinja, sitting by the swamp and gazing at his own reflection, is brought in contact with an apparition — his own arborial destiny — which prefigures the journey he must make in search of divine knowledge. He begins to exemplify the condition which suggests that the tree is an intermediate form of man, since on the one hand it springs from the Primordial Man (the 'trunk' in the creekbed), and on the other it grows into a man. 'As is a tree, just as it is the Lord of Trees, so indeed is man.'[6] Furthermore we are told that the dog is one of the many types of the defender of the Tree of Life.[7] We know, too, that Christ was seen as a tree or vine, and the old Rabbinic idea linked the Tree of Paradise with a man. Thus Ankotarinja's sojourn by the swamp and his vision of the *tnatantja* reaching towards the heavens draws him into a complex metaphysical web denoting

40

numerous aspects of the Dreaming hero as a Tree of Life. This is confirmed by an Ilbalintja tribesman who remarked to Strehlow, 'We northern men have come into being from the primal *tnatantja*'.[8]

Ankotarinja has reached a point where he engages in a new act of sensibility: he breathes deeply and sniffs the four winds. But before we explore the symbolism of the wind, we must consider that in Songs six and seven the *tnatantja* springing from his head is compared with a 'whirlwind'. This alerts us to the idea of a 'tube' of air giving birth to the wind which is highlighted in the Mithraic liturgy where it says, 'And likewise the so-called tube, the origin of the ministering wind. For you will see hanging down from the disc of the sun something that looks like a tube.' This remarkable vision of a tube as represented by the *tnatantja* hanging down from the sun is baffling in a religious text were it not for the fact that the tube has a phallic significance, in that it is the origin of the wind. At first sight the phallic origin is not apparent until we remember that the wind, just as much as the sun, is a fructifier and creator. This is borne out by the ancient superstition which suggests that the mares of Lusitania and Egyptian vultures were fertilized by the wind. More recently, Ezra Pound, the American poet, wrote in his Cantos, 'The wind also is of the process', clearly an allusion to the wind's seminal qualities.

We are therefore confronted with a new image of the process of metaphysical direction. Ankotarinja, in his dog-like capacity ('arinja' means 'dog' in the Aranda language), 'smells' out the warm west wind in preference to the 'cold' winds from the other quarters. He has addressed the four cardinal points, themselves a symbol of the four planes of existence. As explained in the Satapatha Brahmana (III. 6. 4, 12) 'Let him cut the tree from the sacrificial stake so as to fall towards the east, for the east is the quarter of the gods; or to the north, for the north is the quarter of men, or towards the west (the western quarter belongs to the serpents, of wisdom, of sapiential knowledge)'.

Ankotarinja has addressed for the first time the principial

value of self-knowledge as he sniffs out the four planes of manifestation. He has allowed the 'four winds to knit together my parts' as *The Book of the Dead* states. Moreover he rejoices in the scent of the west wind which he says warms his heart. Such a wind is the subject of a Mithraic ritual which states, 'And towards the regions westward it is as though an infinite east wind. But if the other wind should prevail towards the region of the east, you will in like manner see the vision veering in that direction.'[9] The west wind, veering towards the east, becomes a symbol not only of sapiential knowledge, the region of the serpents, but of the underworld. This is confirmed when Ankotarinja 'returns to his place of birth, burning with anger against the west'. In his unrealized, partly chthonic state, he is reluctant to embrace the consequences of his actions. Smelling the warm wind from the west has intimated something to him. He knows that it has something to teach him. At the same time he knows that he will have to give up something — in this case his earthly condition, his self-centredness, his introversion. His anger is a product of loss, of a break with his principal condition. He knows that, like Adam tasting of the fruit of Good and Evil, he must make his journey to the west, out of the Edenic state as symbolized by the creekbed at Ankota, surrounded as it is by its forest of *tnatantjas*.

This act of severance from the past, from his principal condition, is completed when his *tnatantja* falls to the ground. Like the concluding moments of the first act in a play the hero has been born, confronted himself, and acknowledged his destiny. His attempt to 'go back' to his past has failed. He cannot withdraw from the task at hand — that of 'going forward' into the unknown, towards the revelationary landscape in the west. His symbolic head-dress, like the Egyptian *uraeus*, links him to the heavens and to the sun. This falls away from him, and he is left with a vision of his home as a mass of red pebbles on the plains, of sand-ridges, a desert. In a plaintive set of verses we hear him acknowledging that what he believed to be his ideal home no longer existed as he knew it. Ankota had become a wasteland in his eyes. He had stepped out onto the plain of manifestation, confirming once and for all that his pre-existent condition, when he had only been a 'head', a thought, is no more. Instead the west wind lures him towards his destiny. He must set out on the ultimate adventure into the underworld, towards knowledge of eternity and death.

In part Ankotarinja's display of anger at the west wind is as a result of his reluctance to give up what he has attained, the security of the present. He does not want to be drawn forward into the future, towards that divinity which becomes his terror. His anger is inspired by fear as much as his initial aversion to the west wind. Though he may long to return to his hollow, to his world-womb, he instinctively knows that this is impossible. His prevarication echoes that of Hamlet before the ritual murder of the king, his step-father: he knows what he must do but he is unable to bring himself to do it. Like Gilgamesh in the Sumerian epic, he might ask: 'Where is the man who can climb to heaven?' In the end, the decision is taken from him by the magical *tnatantja* which decides to topple from his head. This is the signal that determines his fate. Ankotarinja, like Gilgamesh, must 'follow the sun's road to its rising' if he is ever to realize himself.

We have reached a significant moment in the coming-into-existence of a Dreaming hero. We have followed Ankotarinja's transformation from a inchoate 'thing' lying under the sands of the creekbed at Ankota. Not only has his solar persona been acknowledged, but all the complexities of his mythogenesis serve to emphasize his significance as a creation-hero. He is not just a dog-man, wilful and shiftless, but a supreme exemplar of the demiurge entering into the plane of manifestation. He is an example of the One become Many. It seems that the Aranda people of the Ngala-Mbitjana band have been in possession of an important myth pertaining to the birth of the world. Their rituals, songs and sacred *churinga* form a part of this otherworldy composition. Each is integral to its expression. The myth could not exist without these, nor the land from which Ankotarinja has

43

emerged at the time of the Dreaming. Ankota is the 'stage', the sacred *inkura* ground upon which the drama is played out, both by the Dreaming hero himself and the ritual participants.

In spite of his anger we are left to ponder the pure emptiness of Ankotarinja's mind. Though he thinks, we know he does not think ordinary thoughts. Indeed his thoughts are the great intuitional spread of all ours combined, the wash of images that make up our *anticipation* of what is to follow. We are conscious that he must set out on a subterranean journey. He stands at the entrance to an underground pathway, a cavernous route downwards into the earth. This is the entrance to the underworld, the minotaur's labyrinth, the fosse over which Odysseus must pass. It also represents the 'jaws of death', the snapping together of Agni's 'iron teeth', the Wandering Rocks that bar entrance to the realm of the dead. According to legend every great soul must pass twice through the Gate of Ivory if he is to overcome the cycle of change. Ankotarinja does eventually pass through twice, since he survives his meeting with the *tilpa* men at Parr Erultja and returns. We are aware also that his journey is one that all men must take. The journey he is asking us to accompany him on is designed to transform his myth into an act of mythic transformation for us all. Like him we have quit the realm of ordinary events and embarked upon a luminary voyage in which the dichotomy between right and wrong, good and evil, becomes irrelevant. Ankotarinja has severed the cord binding us to the physical world, to the world of events, to one governed by ethics and law. As yet these do not exist. For Ankotarinja has yet to experience a life where his passions are fully aroused. He is still in that state of innocence, unable to go backwards or forwards.

This is the marvel and subtlety of mythogenesis. In the images of the desert so far encountered around Ankota, we have been brought in contact with a new way of observing ourselves. Like Ankotarinja, the wilful dog in us sniffs the air. We linger over the warm scent drifting in from the west. We are seduced by the prospect of going on an underground journey. At the same time the veil of innocence has fallen away from our eyes.

44

Out of the World-womb

We are now ready to experience the full dimension of passion, evil, and a desire to be reborn. We know what lies ahead of us, at least in its vestigial form. It is time to begin that journey in the company of Ankotarinja, the dog-man who has made the sun his emblem.

CHAPTER 4
The Underground Journey

'No creature can attain a higher grade of nature without ceasing to exist,' wrote Coomaraswamy.[1] This could equally apply to Ankotarinja as he embarks upon his subterranean journey. One is conscious of his precursors: men such as Jonah in the belly of the whale, Gilgamesh on his journey into the mountain of Mashu, Christ to Hell, Odysseus and Aeneas to the underworld, and Dante on his long journey through Purgatory and Hell. The underground journey is a popular image of the life-centering act, and the desire on the part of the hero to enter into a state of transformation. Ankotarinja is no exception to his more recent counterparts. He too has chosen to walk away from the restrictive aspects of his persona in an attempt to realize his essential nature.

We are now entering an entirely new region of symbolism. Though still angry at the west wind ('sucking at his beard as he follows the trail') Ankotarinja continues on the scent trail. He is, in a sense, impassioned, at the mercy of his wilfulness. The anger he feels at being drawn out of himself knows no bounds. He is ready to attack anything that moves. This wolfish nature identifies him with Mars (Ares) since this is the animal of the war-god. His subjugation and transformation will not be easy. But Ares is known to be the prime nature of things, the initiator, the assigner who extends the peculiar nature to all species, and gives individual form.[2] Ankotarinja's dilemma is tied up with his need to transmute his fiery essence into a force that is both intuitive and incorruptible. He must begin to 'name things', empower nature with a life beyond itself. It is at this point that he confronts his other self in the form of the women's footprints which he discovers on the ground at Irbunngurerea. These 'Friday footprints' which seem to imprint on the pristine earth a measure of his aloneness, represent both a primal confrontation with otherness for him and the object which might finally satisfy his passion.

We are told how he 'hungrily' discovers where the women have been digging for frogs in the creek. This alerts us to the fact that these women have a watery character. Not only have they been digging in the creek, but their association with frogs informs us of their 'slippery' nature, and their reputation as custodians of rain.[3] They are water nymphs which, according to Paracelsus, endow Ares (Ankotarinja) with a watery character, thus imbuing him with a spiritual quality for the first time. Like Odysseus, who encounters Nausicaa and her maidens by the washpool in Phaeacia, Ankotarinja is at once brought into contact with a lower, denser region more intimately connected to the body in the form of feminine beauty. Furthermore, we begin to see him as a budding rainmaker, eager to release the fructifying waters onto the parched desert of the inland. We now realize that the dog-man, wolfish in his nature perhaps, is destined for other things. This would concur with his link with the Rainbow Serpent, itself linked to rain and the making of rivers. His mercurial character is now 'on the scent', so to speak, of the Divine Snake in the form of these nymphs who lead him ever deeper into the realm of his self. The fires that he comes upon at their abandoned camps in themselves 'light the way' forward.

When he catches up with the women, we are aware that what follows is no ordinary act of mutilation. The women become aware of his presence in that they 'gaze into the distance, their eyes raised' looking for him. But before this happens Ankotarinja goes through a number of canine motions. It is all part of the ritual of the hunt. The dog-man is creeping up on water-maidens, presumably to quench his 'thirst'. The women's 'sickness' makes them a part of this ritual in that they no longer try to escape. Their sickness may well be linked to their monthly menstrual cycle, which in turn echoes the manifestations of the moon. Their inability to move implies a 'waning', whereby the women present themselves as an offering to Ankotarinja to be born anew. Kitra, the divine Lawgiver, said in the Upanishads (Kaush. I. 2), 'All who depart from this world go to the moon. In the former, (the waxing half), the moon waxes big by their vital [i.e. physical] spirit. But in the waning half, the moon causes them to be born.' It is clear that the frog-maidens are indeed waiting for, rather than escaping from Ankotarinja. They are allowing him to catch up with them, even though the prospect of their encounter with him precipitates fear on their part. Though they are prepared to blame another for their illness, in truth they know they are being prepared for sacrifice.

The next image in this tableau revolves around Ankotarinja's attack on two women in which he bites into their waists. It is a confusing image until one acknowledges the region as being the seat of the liver, and so too of the passionate nature. Prometheus was attacked by an eagle in this part of his anatomy while chained to a mountain in the Caucasus. An obscure woodcut from an alchemical text depicts a wolf attacking the waist of a dead king. The wolf is considered as representing the *prima materia* caught in the act of consuming the *regius filius* or spirit. The idea of only two women being the object of Ankotarinja's interest is echoed in the myth of the Bull of Minos where both Ariadne and her sister, Phaidra, are said to be responsible for leading Theseus from the labyrinth. Ariadne's name means 'holy or pure' with a secondary meaning of 'shining or visible from afar'. Phaidra's, on the other hand, means 'bright'. One is drawn into the context of two women, sisters perhaps, who actually 'attract' Ankotarinja by the strength of their luminosity, their purity. Rather than them being objects to attack on the part of the dog-man, they do in fact offer themselves up to him as a beacon, a sacrifice. They are the principle of otherness that Ankotarinja needs to encounter if he is to go beyond himself. This would concur with the alchemical image of the wolf eating the king: it desires to partake of royalty, the *regius filius*, just as Theseus looked to the light represented by Ariadne and her sister to save him. We are made aware of the fact that Ankotarinja's attack on the women is less a barbaric act than one designed to draw him out of himself, so

49

that he might begin to partake of the feminine.

These women represent 'pairs of opposites' whereby love/ hate, near/far, thick/thin, and so on provide the polarities of the conditional world. It is precisely from these pairs of opposites that liberation must be won; it is from their conflict that Ankotarinja ust escape if he is to be freed from mortality. For him to reach the Farther Shore ('for it is not in space, nor hath it poles': Paradiso XXII. 67) he must not be 'overcome by the pairs' (Maitri Upanishad III. I) nor deluded by the 'mirage of the contrary pairs' which mire him in weal and woe. His journey into the underworld necessitates that he must learn to recognize the fact that he is not alone in this world — that he must partake of another, his feminine half, if he is to re-enter the principial condition once more. These women reflect his 'other half'.

What follows this encounter with the women is the moment when Ankotarinja recognizes the real object of his quest. The *tilpa* men of Parr Erultja stand before him as a progressive delineation of his otherness. The scene that confronts us suggests that Ankotarinja's acts of violence and cannibalism which follow stamp him as a vicious being. But we must be careful not to accept the events as they stand. Strehlow tells us that the *tilpa* men are traditionally regarded as the ancestors who first entered the region from the south. These men are habitually spoken of as *tnenka*, which means 'blood-avengers'. According to Spencer and Gillan these men entered the region at the time of the Dreaming, committing acts of bloodthirsty violence along the way.[4] It so happens that in the ceremonies the white body-paintings they wear represent the murders they were responsible for on the track. In a sense the *tilpa* men represent the 'primitive' hordes that invade the psyche when a man is not yet able to draw upon the protection of custom and law. They are the wild beings that inhabit each one of us before we are able to discern the difference between right and wrong. The *tilpa* men are everything we associate with primordial chaos, the inability to establish a vocational aspect in our lives.

Ankotarinja sees them as a threat. Yet even in this moment

when they lie asleep 'in the midst' of their great *tnatantja*, we begin to encounter the ambivalence of their persona. As foreigners they reflect the anarchic forces of the universe. Yet we notice they are asleep, in a state of oblivion, at one with the Tree of Life. The Brihadaranyaka Upanishad states it thus: 'When now he falls asleep, he takes from this all-comprehending universe the timber, cuts it down, and himself builds up of it his own light, by virtue of his own brilliance; when therefore he sleeps this spirit serves as light for itself.' Ankotarinja is gazing down upon what is at once foreign to his nature, while at the same time intimating the possibility of experiencing a profound transformation of his soul. The *tilpa* men, for all the blood on their hands, are asleep to their past. They too have decided to shelter under the Cosmic Tree, the Tet pillar of Egypt, itself an emblem of the underworld. For the ancient Egyptians such a pillar represented firmness, stability and preservation.[5] It also represents the 'backbone', a sign of aspiration and a willingness to go beyond oneself. The Aborigines clearly see the *tnatantja* in the same light, for they often dance with it tucked into a waistband behind their back, thus emphasizing its 'spinal' nature, its power to support the body.

We must consider the *tnatantja* as an important icon of transcendence. It alone carries within its branches and ceremonial paraphernalia the embodiment of the Aborigine's desire to return to the Dreaming at the time of his death. Like the Crucifix, the Ankh and the Crescent it stands as the primordial recollection of the crossover from this world to the next. It represents the Bridge of Chinvat over which men must pass in order to enter the spiritual world. In the myth of Ankotarinja we have seen how significant the *tnatantja* has been, appearing as it has in every important scene so far. We cannot escape its metaphysical ramifications. That it presides over the 'deep sleep' of the *tilpa* men signals to us what is going on in their minds. They, like Ankotarinja, are engaged in a supreme act of contemplation amid the roots of the *tnatantja*, the Cosmic World Tree itself.

51

Ankotarinja is now bent on consuming the *tilpa* men. Like a 'whirlwind' he snatches them up and swallows them. He begins to align himself with Spirit as it is stated in the Rg Veda (X. 30. 0) where, when 'breath turns resounding up and up' this is called the 're-turn of the spiritual power'[6] which suggests that he has taken back unto himself his primordial powers as an avatar. He is prepared to 'consume' the superficially negative aspect of the *tilpa* men, their blood-avenging propensities which, at a deeper level, reflect their heroic qualities as warriors. Ankotarinja does not eat them out of spite but, like Indra who rushes up to the fallen hero, Vishnu, and swallows him, he is eager to partake of their desirable qualities (Soma) and thus become '*makhavat*, for Makhavat is he who is metaphysically Maghavat — that is, the Sacrifice'.[7] This concurs with the Eucharistic feast where St. John (VI. 56) says: 'He that eateth my flesh and drinketh my blood, dwelleth in me, and I in him'. The blood-avenging habits of the *tilpa* men and the act of cannibalism by Ankotarinja point to the same thing: they all desire to consume the principial virtues of the demiurge as these manifest themselves in the Dreaming heroes. Far from being avengers, it seems that the *tilpa* men come from a distant place (as angelic entities) and have subjected themselves to this act of sacrifice in order that they might expatiate Ankotarinja's initial act of separation (i.e. his coming-into-being) and their own. Their sacrifice becomes a celebration of his manifestation, and theirs, in a way that presides over its incorporation into Aboriginal ritual. The true meaning of cannibalism revolves around an act of expatiation and reintegration, an undoing of the work of disintegration with which the world begins. In swallowing these men, and thus becoming 'fulfilled', he earns the right to lie at the foot of the great *tnatantja*, and so fall into a state of blissful sleep. He has achieved his aim: he has drunk of the spiritual nature (Soma) which is the fruit of the Tree of Life, and thereby absorbed the mystic virtue of sacrifice. The Aborigines call this spiritual substance *kurunba* which is a part of all ritual objects, as well as the sacred *inkura* ground where the Dreaming events were said to have originated.

Another Dreaming hero now comes upon Parr Erultja from the west. Though he is not named, we sense that he is endowed with a personality of his own. Travelling alone, it seems that he is familiar with the *tilpa* men, that they are perhaps his blood-brothers. It appears that he comes from a far place, from a world that is not yet manifest. He also observes that the west wind no longer blows from its sacred source (over which he has custodial powers), nor are the *tilpa* men, the guardians of the great *tnatantja*, there to welcome him. All is silent. Parr Erultja has become like a graveyard. It is as though a fatal disruption to the cosmic order is being intimated. However integral Ankotarinja's act of cannibalism is to himself — at another level, a more principial level again, its significance sends shockwaves throughout the world. The man from the west makes us aware that all Ankotarinja's actions so far bear the mark of a pathological dilemma: the spirit's desire to become manifest while at the same time wishing to remain veiled. He, Ankotarinja, is a wounded spirit-being. In spite of his desire for reintegration, he has now distanced himself from principial innocence.

In this sense we can identify with Ankotarinja more than at any other moment of his travail. His blissful sleep is laden with all the weight of unconsciousness, in spite of what has so far occurred. While at one level he partakes of the great *tnatantja*, at another he is seen as a monster. Blind, lacking eyes altogether, he takes on the garb of all heroes who set out on a quest and ultimately fail. His persona echoes that of Oedipus at Colonus, hedged in by his own sightlessness, yet 'insightful' nevertheless. The blind seer, Tiresius, also comes to mind. To the man from the west, however, Ankotarinja is a monster, a failed being who still manages to 'gleam red in the firelight'. His solar qualities remain intact even in sleep. Ankotarinja is still light-filled, still 'inspired', in spite of his monstrous nature. We must remember that Cronus swallowed his sons and daughters in an attempt to prevent his own dethronement. Likewise, Ankotarinja has eaten the *tilpa* men in his attempt to assure his own continuity. He represents the old order of spirit-beings struggling with a new, more vigorous group 'from the west'. The man from the west is like Zeus, ready to destroy his father and so initiate a new order. His thunderbolt (lightning) turns out to be none other than a *churinga*, the sacred word of the Dreaming which he uses as a weapon. More than anything he wishes to release the *tilpa* men from their imprisonment within the belly of the monster. For these beings are now synonymous with Jonah in the belly of the whale. They have encountered 'mighty mysteries' (Paracelsus) which are said to be like a pearl of illumination hanging suspended in the whale's belly. Clearly the man from the west wishes to release these 'illuminations' in the form of the *tilpa* men imprisoned inside Ankotarinja. The mystery Ankotarinja holds within himself represents the stock of primordial images that everyone possesses as his birthright.

The man from the west's anger represents the divine anger of containment. Ultimately the message of the Dreaming cannot be contained. It may remain veiled as it so often does behind a wall of secrecy within the rituals themselves, but the truth of it may be revealed in accordance with strict, initiatory guidelines. These constitute the law for Aborigines, a corpus of belief handed down to them from and by the Dreaming heroes themselves. It is up to the elders of the tribe to draw forth from Ankotarinja's belly what truths the Dreaming has to offer. While at one level the man from the west's approach of the 'monster' on his hands and knees suggests that he sees Ankotarinja as his potential prey; at another, his actions suggest a more reverential demeanour in the presence of the Dreaming hero. Ankotarinja is both dead to the world, a monster and an icon embodying all the virtues of insight and glory which are attributable to a person from the otherworld.

The man from the west is on his hands and knees before the sun itself. Ankotarinja is like the brazen dog that was appointed as one of Europa's guardians. He is the monstrous/magical creature known as Talos, the giant who wandered about an island (the world) twice daily. Talos was reputed to have only one vulnerable spot, a vein running from the nape of his neck to his knuckle. His name, in the Cretan language, means the Sun. Thus the man from the west found himself approaching the Divine Sun manifesting itself as the golden or 'red' dog. By attacking him with a *churinga* stone — that is, the word or law — one senses that the man from the west represents the new order of humankind attempting to 'lay low' or at least codify the generative powers of the sun. If this can be harnessed, then humankind will be able to embark upon a life on this earth with at least some measure of protection. So that for a short while, at least in mythopoeic terms, the subject of the Ankotarinja myth becomes the man from the west. He is transformed into the hero, the slayer of dragons, the prototype of St George. He takes it upon himself to bring down the solar attributes of Ankotarinja which threaten to 'burn up' the world. Water, after all, is the one element all in life thirsts for. By aiming the law at the sun, he is directing the 'spear that never missed' to its target. In his hands the sacred *churinga* becomes a magical weapon of retribution — and resolution.

The man from the west hurls the *churinga* at Ankotarinja's one vulnerable point — the nape of his neck. At once the head of the monster rolls away, allowing the *tilpa* men who have been swallowed to be disgorged. We hear that they 'flowed forth like water' — a fitting aftermath to the solar excesses which cause drought, aridity and death. The *tilpa* men are water-bringers, rain, and are of course kinsfolk to the frog-women who were attacked earlier in the myth. They have been released onto a parched world by the law — that is, proper ritual invocation has brought about rain. It is clear from this act alone that the *churinga* represents the importance of sacred ritual and the correct procedural use of ceremony in the renewal of the world. No wonder the Aborigines regard their *churinga* as their only protection against the forces of dissimulation and anarchy. They represent the Tablet, the supreme coda of existence. Without them the world would become a parched place, a desert. It is fitting that Ankotarinja should be the bearer of all things, all beneficence, since he is the avatar.

The *tilpa* men climb up onto the rocky hills, and swing their bullroarers merrily. Like rain they are making noises in the gullies and in the creeks. Decorating their heads with green twigs and wallaby tails signifies the rebirth of the world after a deluge. Plants sprout, seed materializes, animals give birth. Everywhere there is a sense of growth as the earth breaks out of its parched prison. We know, for example, that Namuci ('Holdfast') was a Pharaoh who would not let his people go, nor release the Waters.[8] Like the Serpent, Vtra ('Enveloper', or 'Roller'), Susna (Sirocco, Drought), Ankotarinja represents in his sacrificial aspect the source from which all things flow forth. When Vtra was decapitated, Soma or the life-sap flowed from him. The rolling away of Ankotarinja's head from his trunk reflects an extroversion, a turning or revolution of nature, an embodiment of the 'wheel of becoming'. Furthermore his orphidic nature aligns him with the activities of the Great Snake, the Water Spirit. His decapitation reflects a disenchantment of the victim, and a liberation of the Sun from the darkness by which he had been obscured and eclipsed. Ankotarinja's sacrificial death is a making of Many into One again. His dismemberment is a consummation desired by the victim himself in order that all the imprisoned principles are released. 'When he had emanated all beings, [he] felt himself emptied out, as it were, and was afraid of death: he bethought himself. "How can I get these beings back into myself.... How can I come to be again the Self of all these beings?"' (Satapatha Brahmana). It is well known that the express purpose of the Sacrifice, as a rite enacted and to be comprehended, is to build up again, at one and the same time the sacrificer's and the deity's Self, whole and complete. This in turn duplicates the labours of the Year undertaken by the hero.

The myth of Ankotarinja spins out a tale that is simultaneous and eternal. The dog-man is, for once, quietened by his slaughterer, though he is really liberated or disenchanted, like so many other enchanted princes who must be beheaded before they can put off the animal forms in which they are imprisoned.

The decapitation of this outlandish and uncanny stranger does not signal his death, however. In fact, what it does signal is the inevitable denouement in which Ankotarinja's head 'rolls back' to its origin. The victor, in this case the man from the west, must submit himself to the immortal victim, the dog-man from Ankota. To understand this paradox we must know that the Sacrifice, by which the One is made Many, although a willing self-sacrifice which reflects Ankotarinja's desire to be multiplied and divided, insofar as it is performed by the Dreaming hero from the west and submitted to by the Victim, implicates them both in an 'original sin' from which all parties shrink. Expiation must take place sooner or later so that the process of redemption can be realized.

The final purpose of the Sacrifice is not merely to continue the creative process that occurred at the time of the Dreaming when this first decapitation came about, but also to reverse it by building up again the divided Dreaming hero so that he might be whole and complete once more. Ankotarinja must be re-assembled by those who divided him. If his sacrifice does not involve both an act of disintegration and one of reintegration it cannot serve, as it so clearly does, 'for the winning of *both* worlds' (Taittiriya Samita). 'The head of the Sacrifice [must be] put on again' (SB). 'It will not suffice us that the Sacrifice has been taken to pieces; come, let us gather it together again' (Aitareya Brahmana). We are dealing here with a need on the part of Ankotarinja and the *tilpa* men to acknowledge their contingency as participants in the rite of sacrifice. As a result their roles are inherited by the songmen and dancers who enact the myth at ceremonial moments.

The severed head of the monster rebounds and continues to rebound to this day in the form of the sun. We know this to be true as we have already ascertained Ankotarinja's solar attributes. His head becomes a living sacrifice which rolls back to its birthplace. It follows in the path of the head 'rolling towards our field' which knows the nature of the 'hidden mystery'[9] as Rumi states. This mystery is none other than the self-naughting, self-abandoning process by which the self seeks renewal. Among Native Americans, the severed head is described as a 'rolling rock', just as in the Rg Veda it is described as a 'bright revolving rock'. Ankotarinja's head is the sun returning to its birthplace in the east, there to be 're-born' on the following morning. The final song confirms this fact when it likens his head to the 'heart of a flame of fire'. His redness is none other than the dawning sun overreaching the world once more.

We are at last back where we commenced our journey — in the dry watercourse near Ankota. It seems strange to think that we have survived such a torrid encounter with the underworld. It is even more remarkable to think that what appeared impenetrable at the onset turned out to be so rich in connotation. Ankotarinja, the dog-man and Solar hero, rainmaker and Serpent-man, seemed to shed so many skins of revelation en route to his ultimate homeland. More importantly, perhaps, he led us far from the familiar world of contingency in which we normally feel so at home. In the process we have managed to regain our state of pristine recognition through the act of gazing into this mysterious realm of mythogenesis. The myth of Ankotarinja has drawn our attention to the importance of recognizing that our immortal self has its seat in our head, and our mortal self in the trunk. The return of the Sacrificial Head to its place of abode confirms what we already know: that the pilgrimage is significant for the pilgrim only until he reaches its end, until he 'goes home'. Its implication for Aborigines, and ourselves, is clear: to 'turn back' is to repent, to undergo conversion. This reversion of the spiritual power is coincident with the rising of the Sun, whether at Ankota or within ourselves.

The Aborigines of Central Australia have found a unique way of expressing Ankotarinja's message, both in ceremony and in their ritual art. The 'dot-art' method of expression in painting is also confined to this region of the world. The patterns, the rhythms and the whorls that are created on the earth are not all that dissimilar to those that appear in Celtic art or among that of other traditional peoples who rely on repetition as the basis for their aesthetic. This art-form is hieratic in context, and so does not conform to humanist aspirations based upon the need for visual or sensual recognition. The paintings represent 'spiritual topography' and so map perfectly a metaphysical landscape. Each dot painting found on an *inkura* ground reflects the journey of the Dreaming hero. It also reflects the mythogenic experience whereby the Divine Question is announced. To gather around a dot painting on the ground is to become, as an individual, one dot among all the other individual dots that go to make up the myth-event itself. These dots are soul-centred, the incarnation of mythic knowledge which continues to defy any attempt to analyse its content. The myth is engaged in a constant battle to resist such analysis, since not to do so would imply a lack of *kurunba*, and therefore a diminution of the possibility of realizing its theophanic significance.

What begins to emerge from such an encounter is that the participants are themselves adjuncts to the mythogenic experience. Ankotarinja cannot survive without their input, just as they cannot survive without his glorious appearance in the world. Each time his ceremonies are performed he becomes responsible for granting them renewed contact with the Dreaming, with the great mystery of creation, multiplicity and death. Without his numinous presence within their midst the Aborigines of Central Australia would find themselves devoid of an avatar, and so reduced to the level of *tilpa* men — that is wanderers on this earth, with no prospect of ever reaching home. Ankotarinja has opened the way for all humankind to make an underground journey in search of answers and return again victorious along the same route. He has given men the chance to 'glow like the heart of a fire', to experience gnosis, to curl up in the sacred hollow of earth knowledge like a wild dog. His propensity to sniff out the truth is well attested, for this dog-man has made it his business to follow its trail beyond the realm of manifestation into that subterranean cavern where the great *tnatantja* stands upright, a symbol of the 'Still Heart' awaiting the transmutation of its mortal condition.

Part ll:
By Muruwul Waterhole

CHAPTER 5
The Sacred Mother Sings

In the northern region of Australia a sacred cult known as Kunapipi preserves the mythogenic reality of the Sacred Mother, the perpetually pregnant woman. On the one hand she is regarded as a fertility figure; on the other, she is linked to the Rainbow Serpent as a symbol of abundance and renewal. Often called the 'Old Woman', she is responsible for the fertility of humankind, all natural species, the sequence of the seasons and the growth of all vegetable and plant life. She invented sacred ritual also. As well, she encourages the traditional pattern of society, the law, religious thought and speculation. Indeed Kunapipi herself highlights the maternal, nourishing, reproductive and creative principle in nature and in humankind. She represents the principle ground of being, the earth-womb or *nongaru*.

To talk of her is to engage in a dialogue with all the mothers of the world. Her form may be that of the many-breasted Diana of Ephesus, a plump effigy vessel from Minonian Crete or the goddess Nut overreaching the sky. She may be Kali, Rati or Venus. Whatever her image, Kunapipi embodies a principle of fecundity that transcends all her many manifestations. She is both female in her creative, nurturing phase, and male in her seminal, ordering phase. Combining mysteriously with the Rainbow Serpent, we see vulva and phallus merge into one generative organ in her being. Like the lingam (phallus) in which the figure of the goddess is carved in Hindu sculpture, the principle of duality achieves unity. Male and female become one in the deity's image, in this case Shiva's. Kunapipi's numinosity is derived from an underlying belief in the idea that her avid womb attracts the male and kills the phallus within itself in order to achieve satisfaction and fecundation.

To enter the realm of Kunapipi is to enter a terrain of

timeless antiquity. Her mythogenic presence permeates the thought and belief of the northern tribes, and in turn filters outward into the cosmogonies of many southern and western peoples. Across the land there is a sense of a vast, inchoate femininity at work within the earth. The seasonal monsoon rains, the barren months prior to the advent of summer storms, the sense of growth and renewal after long periods of drought — all these natural events are a reflection of Kunapipi's character. As the Old Woman she is both salacious and cantankerous, matriarchal and maternal. She is the terrible creature known to the Malekula people of the Pacific as Le-hev-hev, she who 'draws us to It so that It may devour us.'[1] She is also Kali. Moreover her uroboric bi-sexuality determines her role as a guardian spirit of the underworld and the annihilating influence of the grave.

When we encounter her myth we encounter a figure much larger than the shadowy, pendulous figure which we sometimes see depicted in Aboriginal bark paintings, or in the extended vulvas carved into rock on various cave walls. Her physical attributes do indeed embody all of these characteristics, but she is also much more. Kunapipi embraces the feminine as a vessel of rebirth and higher transformation. She is Sophia, the 'spirit and the bride' of the Apocalypse, the process by which all things are spiritualized by the 'living waters' that she represents. Kunapipi is essential womanhood whose true form can only be imagined by way of ritual and ceremony, since in her embodiment as the Old Woman she does not have any recognizable features. Like Ankotarinja she is a spirit-entity. Her visage is made up of sublime action, not those normal features which might identify her with a human prototype.

Therefore we must look to a myth which embodies all her actions, remembering of course that as a spirit-entity she inhabits every aspect of the myth rather than posing as a character within the myth itself. Kunapipi is both the Great Mother in the form of a whispered act of reverence, as well as being all songs, ritual movements, even the sacred ground upon which the ceremony is enacted, the body-paintings and indeed the participants who recreate her image in the world. Her physical persona takes on a hieratic dimension consistent with all the activities of mimesis. She has no manifest qualities except those of absence. She is the invisible presence of a fecund principle working through a mythic repertoire known only to the initiated, to the men of knowledge. In her eternal loving embrace as the 'redeeming one' Kunapipi holds the maleness of the Rainbow Serpent to her bosom, so that his unapproachability becomes immersed in her.

It is important to identify these values before embarking upon an explanation of the myth itself. Once we enter her mythic realm we will have confronted images that are inexplicable in terms of human behaviour. By the time the Kunapipi songs have become a part of our consciousness, we too will have entered into the deep abysm of death and rebirth. The bullroarer will have been sounded, sending forth flashes of lightning ('like the tongue of the Snake') to frighten off the uninitiated. The *nongaru* ground (ritual environment) will have been prepared, symbol of the Snake and the divine uterus combined. The participants will have anointed themselves with those images designed to set them apart from mundane reality. They will have taken on the garb of their totemic heroes, their 'other selves' as they begin to detach themselves from what makes them most human. This is the moment when the Wauwalak Sisters will emerge from the primordial waters of the myth in order to do battle with the Rainbow Serpent, Julungul. It is the moment when the Divine Mother manifests herself in all her terrible yet pristine aspects. As Brahma prays to the Great Goddess, 'Thou art the ultimate nature and the clear light of heaven, which illuminates and breaks the self-hypnotism of the terrible round of rebirth, and thou art the one who muffles the universe, for all time in thine own very darkness,'[2] so too will the spirit of Kunapipi begin to emerge from her own 'very darkness' on the sacred *nongaru* ground.

We are fortunate that a then young and enterprising anthropologist named Ronald Berndt chose to begin his research into the Kunapipi myth (in the 1940s) at a time when the Aboriginal culture of the North was still vigorous. He was able to record the song-cycles and events of the Wauwalak Sisters myth when its spiritual significance was still strongly felt among the people. Though he was unable to extrapolate the primordial significance of Kunapipi, he nonetheless drew our attention to the profound importance of her role. In his book *Kunapipi* he made us aware of the complex relationship between myth, ritual, and song among the Yirrkala people of northeast Arnhem Land. These people, whose traditional home camps are around Blue Mud Bay, Trial and Caledon Bays and Port Bradshaw to the south, facing the Gulf of Carpentaria, had already come in contact with Methodist missionaries. However, he found that this veneer of Christianity did not inhibit belief in Kunapipi, nor did church ceremony prevent them from fulfilling their ritual obligations on behalf of the Great Mother.

The Kunapipi myth is not indigenous to the northern part of Australia. According to Berndt[3] the myth travelled from the south along the Roper River system. On the way, it met up with a much older myth-cycle known as Djangawul, himself a fertilizing Dreaming hero of supreme importance. Djangawul had two sisters with whom he engaged in incestuous activity at the time of the Dreaming. He regularly pushed aside their extended clitori and placed his hand in their wombs in order to draw forth the ancestors of the Aborigines and disperse them across the land. The arrival of the Kunapipi myth from the south precipitated a merging of certain key elements with the older Djangawul myth material, the most important feature being the transformation of Djangawul's sisters into the Wauwalak Sisters. These sisters, though they arrived from the south, soon found themselves incestuously pregnant in imitation of the Djangawul sisters they had transposed. The newer myth-cycle from the south merged with the older one from the north, bringing together the two motifs of the Pregnant Mother with that of the World Creator.[4]

Djangawul's place of origin was the island of Bralgu, the Land of the Dead or the Land of the Eternal Beings. The island lay off the coast of Arnhem Land. This was not his primary point of origin, however, since the Aborigines believe that he and his sisters came from an unknown land beyond Bralgu. Bralgu was a transit place en route to Australia which, at the time of the Dreaming, was considered to be unpeopled. Only birds, animals, trees and fish inhabited the land, rivers and coastal regions. Djangawul, with his elongated penis and his two sisters with their extended clitori, populated the land with their myriad offspring. Whether their arrival echoes the appearance of the original migrants from Southeast Asia prior to the first Ice-age is unclear. But it does seem that Djangawul's party duplicated the arrival of Paleolithic peoples countless millennia before. On the available evidence this event may be dated approximately 50,000 years ago. But it could have been even earlier. The important point to observe is that Djangawul's arrival implies a myth of immense age. He came over from Bralgu 'before time' — that is, in the age of the Dreaming.

While Kunapipi means 'Old Woman' or 'Mother' to the Yirrkala people, it is also said to refer to the Rainbow Serpent[5] which swallowed the Wauwalak Sisters as described in the myth. The word has other connotations, namely 'whistle-cock' or penis sub-incision, a practice popular among Roper River tribes. Ritually splitting the penis occurs throughout Australia during ceremonies on fully initiated men as a sign of their progress toward knowledge. Its origin lies in what Coomaraswamy calls the bi-section of the serpent as a sign 'of the diremption [forcible separation] of Heaven and Earth'[6]. In other words, the Divine Person bisected himself, thus dividing the male and female principles which until then had been one androgynous unity. Sub-incision is a symbolic expression of the schism by which Sky separates from the Earth, the Knower from the Known, and in general of all the pairs of opposing tensions or values that make up the material world. It also invokes the separation of the 'two selves' which dwell together in us, respectively mortal and immortal. By cutting the penis, the Aborigine acknowledges the primordial unity becoming manifest as the 'pairs of opposites' in order that it might become whole again through ritual activity. In the act of cutting his penis he is recreating female genitalia as a part of his own, and so signalling their primodial unity.

The unification of the male-female principle in the name of Kunapipi suggests another aspect of Djangawul symbolism. It is said that Djangawul represents the principle of unity known as *Jutu'indi*, which in turn was divided into two tribal clan-systems, known as moieties, at the time of the Dreaming. Djangawul, who was of the *dua* moiety, created the *jiritja* moiety, thus instituting the concept of metamorphosis into the realm of humanity. All marriage activity among Aborigines revolves around the correct observance of *dua-jiritja* relationships. In terms of the myth itself, it seems that *dua*-related themes such as that of Djungawul and the Wauwaluk Sisters fall into the category of indigenous belief, and are therefore considered to be the more sacred. Whereas those beliefs that have been imported from elsewhere, namely Indonesia, fall into the *jiritja* or 'outside' category.

Such a view finds its echo in a Rg Veda story of the Arya and Deva which relates how the Aryans were the first people to 'cross the waters' (cf. the Djangawul party voyaging from Bralgu) and settle round the 'Light'. By analogy these people may be compared with the *dua* moiety, and their counterparts, the Deva, with the *jiritja* moiety. We are all Aryans (*dua*) by father-right and Deva (*jiritja*) on the mother-side. The feminine principle is always Deva/*jiritja*, the masculine Arya/*dua*, which reaffirms the Vedas' exhortation that humankind are 'children of the night and day', of 'water and fire'. Our very existence is derived from an exogamy and a miscegenation — that is, a mixing of races — thereby inheriting a bilateral symmetry in accordance with the 'right and left' eyes of Indra and Indrani as detailed in the Upanishads. Eve, the 'mother of all living', is born from Adam's side. It follows that in the *dua/jiritja* duality we have a remnant of the principial gesture of unity (*Jutu'indi*) towards multiplicity at the time of world-creation (Dreaming).

The Sacred Mother Sings

The Kunapipi ceremonies are normally held in the dry season when food is plentiful. The Aborigines are reaping the benefit of the performances of the previous year, while at the same time they are preparing for the coming wet season and the subsequent growth of new food sources. The ceremonies often extend over a period ranging from two weeks to two months, and sometimes even as long as two years. The principal Kunapipi leader is usually a man whose totemic objects and stories are associated with the sacred well from which the Wauwalak Sisters were said to have first emerged. He is invariably of the *dua* moiety, though this does not mean that *jiritja* clan-members do not take part in the ceremonies. The Kunapipi ceremonies, after all, are part of an age-grading ritual for the younger men, of which *jiritja* novitiates are equally involved. In any event they represent the Jiritja snakes (male) which live in the same waterhole as the Rainbow Serpent, Julungul, who is female.

A sacred ground in the shape of a triangle is prepared in the bush, some distance from camp. A man swings a bullroarer to signal the beginning of the ceremony. A hush follows throughout camp as people (men and women) hear the deep-throated sound of Julungul calling to them. At once the women cry out, their plaints like those of the Wauwaluk Sisters waiting for Julungul to sneak up on them. Almost immediately after this the *jiritja* men accompany the young boys 'to meet Julungul' at the sacred ground. The boys are smeared with red-ochre and arm blood. As far as the women are concerned their disappearance from camp means that they have been 'swallowed by the Snake'. In theory, they are not supposed to return to the society of women until they are reborn at the end of the Kunapipi ceremonies. The older men will be responsible to 'chase the Snake back' to its sacred waterhole (the *nongaru* ground) in order to avert the disaster of the entire camp being swallowed by Julungul.

The symbolic rite of exclusion is designed to prolong the personality of the participants beyond a point where they think purely in terms of physical causality. By placing themselves within the field of the *nongaru* ground, they give up their

69

individual will and so find themselves 'released' by the performance of the rite. The environment in its totality is thus changed, prefiguring a merging of the present with the future. All states of being are thereby seen as being simultaneously in the eternal now. For the Aborigine this preliminary rite of mimetic magic is an enactment of the 'formal cause' of all subsequent ritual activity. The *nongaru* ground becomes a place where a man realizes his inheritance as a part of nature. He sees his life in terms of images, each one of which allows him insight into a higher world.

Later that evening the men return to camp, having left the boys in the protection of their guardians. Their message to the women, and particularly the mothers, is that 'Julungul has swallowed them all up.' The women begin to wail, singing the clan songs of the initiates as if they were dead. In theory, at least, the women should not cry for 'they might become sick', since Julungul might grow angry, believing that the women did not agree with her methods. In other words, Julungul 'might return and swallow them up too.' The stage is now set for the enactment of the Kunapipi rites which celebrate the encounter between the Rainbow Serpent and the Wauwalak Sisters at the legendary Muruwul waterhole, represented in the rite by the sacred *nongaru* ground. Into this 'great hole' all the animals, birds and vegetables, in the guise of totemic actors, enter in order to dance out the myth.

The Kunapipi rites are central to the enactment of the myth of the Wauwalak Sisters. What follows is a series of ritual gestures designed to introduce the younger men to the emergence of Julungul 'from the waters' — that is, the fountainhead from which all the powers of the world-soul come forth to create a 'river of beings' (Rumi: *The Divan of Shems of Tabriz*). In the process, the Yirrkala people become emulators of the world-creating activity inherent in this encounter between the sisters and the snake. The primordial landscape of northern Australia is drawn into a pageant of otherworldly dimension: animals, birds, vegetation and humankind wear the ceremonial garb of all Creation as they enact the mythogenic experience of world-birth. They become cohorts as they journey towards that moment when unity reigns. Ultimately Kunapipi presides over a process by which the Many becomes One again.

We are now ready to explore in depth the myth of the Wauwalak Sisters. These two spirit-women bear upon their frail shoulders a causative moment in the history of the world. They live within us too as the Divine Virgin, even when we discover that at least one of them has borne a child. Already we are aware that they inhabit a region of our minds where the nurturing instinct is paramount. Incest, cannibalism and regurgitation will be important motifs, or course. At the beginning we will see the primeval goddess, Kunapipi, resting in the materiality of her elementary character, knowing nothing but the secret of her womb. Her illuminatory power is no gift or flash of light from above; it is a living growth which has taken root in the depths of the earth and is fed by the numinous waters of life. Her incarnation is the incarnation of the Eternal Feminine which unfolds in the history of humankind as in the history of every individual woman. Her self-revelation in the guise of the Wauwalak Sisters prefigures her role as the Lady of Plants and Animals, the genetrix of the spirit as Sophia, the self-unfolding of the feminine nature itself.[7] At this point let us plunge into Muruwul waterhole in the hope of re-emerging in the guise of all the Dreaming heroes and spiritual exemplars that have so far graced the interworld of nature on our behalf.

CHAPTER 6
The Wauwalak Sisters

The myth of the Wauwaluk Sisters is rarely told in prose by story-tellers among the Yirrkala people. According to Berndt, it is normally transmitted from one group of men to another, from generation to generation, using ritual, and accompanied by explanations on the ceremonial *nongaru* ground. The entire myth is usually related as esoteric information embedded in a cycle of some hundreds of songs linked to the bush and to the sea. There are two separate song-cycles which are esoteric in content, as well as an exoteric or secular corpus of songs which can be sung by the women back at camp. Each one of these song-sequences reflects the very best in Aboriginal poetry. It is as if the ancient lays of epic poetry that we find in India, Assyria, Greece and in Norse mythology derive their origin from these elaborate and often repetitive song-cycles from northern Australia. Indeed it seems that all of Aborigine religious aspirations are expressed in this remarkable mythopoem.

The myth begins:

The Wauwalak Sisters, one older than the other, decided to quit their homeland, known as the land of the *dua*. It may have been because the elder sister had engaged in an incestuous relationship with a clansman and fallen pregnant. As a result she was known as Gungman — that is a 'mature, child-bearing woman.' Her younger sister was known as Wirlkul, meaning 'having no child.'

The two sisters travelled in the direction of the sacred waterhole of Muruwul. On the way they named all the animals, birds, and plants. Each carried a stone spear, and wore decorative headbands made from feathers and cane armlets. The younger sister, Wirlkul, wore a breast girdle of woven fibre which crossed under her swelling breasts. As they walked along they killed lizards, possums, bush rats, and kangaroos for food. They also dug for yams. These they placed in a large dilly-bag, saying, "You will become *mareiin* (an exoteric term denoting 'sacred') later." It appears that these would

The Waulwalak Sisters

in turn become *rangga* (an esoteric term for 'sacred') objects and be commemorated in ceremony.

The women eventually reached a place called Gruawona where the younger sister suggested they rest. The older sister agreed since she could already feel her child moving within her womb. So they made a fire and rested here. Within a short while the elder sister gave birth to a baby girl who belonged to the *jiritja* moiety — in spite of the fact that her father had been a *dua* clansman like her mother, as a result of their incestuous union. The sisters remained at Gruawona until the mother had recovered. It appeared that she still bled a little whenever she walked about. When Gungman and her child were well enough to move, the party continued their journey toward Muruwul waterhole. However Gungman's bleeding had not completely stopped, so that a trail of blood had been left at intervals along the track. When they reached Muruwul they made a fire, and produced some food from the dilly-bag which they cooked.

First they placed the possum on the fire to roast. As soon as the creature grew warm it came back to life and ran off. Then they tried to cook the bandicoot, but it too rose from the fire and escaped. The same pattern of behaviour occurred when they placed the lizard, rat and other animals on the fire.

It so happened that in the sacred waterhole lived a great *dua* rock python known as Julungul. She was said to be the boss of all the animals, birds and vegetables in the region. In the same pool other male snakes were said to live also. But Julungul was regarded as *jindibapi* or 'big snake' because of her size.

It appears that the animals which had risen from the sisters' fire knew they were in the vicinity of Julungul's haven, and that it was forbidden to eat nearby. The proximity of food to the pool made the food itself sacred and therefore taboo to the sisters. They knew further that Gungman's bleeding has desecrated the waterhole, an act which was sure to arouse the ire of Julungul. The animals recognized that there was 'big business' in the pool which made it a sacred place. It seems that the sisters should have camped some distance away.

Leaving the fire, the animals ran to the waterhole and jumped in. In doing so they were to become *mareiin* (sacred) and therefore future *rangga* objects. This act of jumping in the pool was designed to indicate to the women that the place was taboo, and that it was against the law to cook or sit near it. Unfortunately the women were not aware of the mistake they had made.

The Waulwalak Sisters

Meanwhile two small edible snakes known as *gundaru*, similar to Julungul, ran down to the pool and jumped in. These snakes were really *gulpanwa*, meaning 'yellow snake'.

The Wauwalak Sisters became uneasy. As soon as they tried to roast their yams, these too burnt to ashes when they were placed on the fire. "They made themselves into ashes," one remarked. It was true; their spirits had left the fire and gone to the sacred waterhole.

"What's wrong with this place?" one younger women asked. "Something strange is happening. All the animals and yams have disappeared. What will we do? Should we sleep here?"

"We'll sleep here," the elder woman replied. "It's all right."

"What's that?" the younger woman said, believing she had heard a noise emanating from Muruwul.

"It's a very deep pool," said the older woman. "We'll sleep nearby, anyway."

Unknowingly Wirlkul had already heard the submarine movements of Julungul as she slowly emerged from the waterhole. It appeared that all the animals and yams had disturbed her slumber as they jumped into the pool. She had smelt the blood of the elder sister too. Raising her head from the water, her nostrils quivering, Julungul at once sprayed a great fountain of water into the air which formed into rainclouds.

The Wauwalak Sisters, who were huddled together, noticed these clouds forming. But they did not suspect that Julungul had sent them.

"It's going to rain," Gungman said to her younger sister. "You'd better gather some stringy bark so that we can make a shelter."

"All right, sister," Wirlkul said, leaving camp to cut sheets of bark. Gungman, after all, was still too weak to do heavy work.

When Wirlkul had gathered sufficient bark, the two women began the task of building a shelter. Then they built a fire near the entrance before climbing inside to rest. By this time the sun had gone down and the rain had begun to fall. Soon the rivulets had washed the coagulated blood from the ground into the sacred well. Again Julungul stirred. She was greatly disturbed by the sight of blood floating above her.

Meanwhile, after it was dark, Julungul again emerged from the waterhole. Holding her head high, she spat out lightning, one vivid flash after another. Thunder rolled. The Wauwalak Sisters awoke and hugged one another in fear. Each time they saw lightning flash they called out. The flashes they saw were different to any other lightning they had ever seen, yet they did not know that Julungul

75

The Waulwalak Sisters

was its cause. They thought it had come from the clouds.

Julungul slowly and deliberately dragged her sinuous body out of the sacred waterhole. The lightning ceased. The sisters were relieved that the storm had ended. Still they had not seen Julungul.

Gradually the Great Snake slid towards the clearing where the sisters and the child were camped. As she approached the shelter, her eyes protruding like search-lights, she tried to locate the women. Suddenly the sisters recognized Julungul lying there before them. They cried out, hoping to frighten her away.

"What are we going to do?" Wirlkul asked.

"We'd better dance to keep her at bay," replied Gungman.

So Wirlkul began to dance in an attempt to hinder the Snake's progress. She moved gracefully, shuffling her feet, swaying her body from side to side. In her hands she held feathered string from which she made cats'-cradles while she danced. She called out, "*Kei'wa! Kei'wa!*" which means "Go away! Go away!" Julungul stopped in her course to watch the dancing. Eventually Wirlkul grew tired and called to her sister, "It's your turn now. I need to rest."

Gungman left her child in its cradle of paperbark, and began to dance near their shelter. As she did so more blood began to flow. At once Julungul smelt the blood and moved toward them both.

"Sister, it's better that you dance rather than me," Gungman announced. "I'm bleeding again, and the Snake has smelt it. She is coming closer."

So Wirlkul took her sister's place and resumed dancing in an attempt to stop Julungul coming forward. But Julungul gazed at the shelter, her eyes never moving. From time to time she breathed out lightning flashes. In this way the two women were forced to take it in turns to dance. Julungul always came nearer each time Gungman danced. So Wirlkul did most of the dancing, swaying from side to side until all this activity caused her own menstruation to begin. Julungul smelt the blood and at once slithered forward.

The Wauwalak Sisters immediately retreated into their shelter. Julungul drew nearer, coiling her body around the outside. Then she put her head inside and sprayed the two women and the child with her saliva in order to make them slippery. The mysterious substance known as *ngeiakngeiakma* soon made their bodies soft all over. Now they were ready to be swallowed whole. Julungul opened her great mouth and ate first the child, then Gungman. Even as she was being swallowed, her breast still protruding from the snake's mouth, Gungman cried out "Go away! Go away!" But Julungul took

76

The Waulwalak Sisters

no notice. She then swept up Wirlkul and swallowed her too.

Well satisfied, Julungul slowly returned to Muruwul waterhole. As she entered the water, she suddenly stood erect, her head upright and high out of the water, a massive pillar of strength. Then she slowly contracted into the water again, to disappear below the surface into that shadowy realm where her husband, also known as Julungul, was waiting for her.

Later, when Julungul had crawled onto the bank again to digest her meal in the sun, she suddenly vomited up the two sisters and the child. "Maybe I've swallowed my own sisters and my daughter," she thought.

The morning sun began to dry out the inert bodies lying on the ground. Soon a trail of ants had reached them and begun to drink the blood in their veins. The ants bit into the sisters. At once they flinched and moved about. Julungul watched what was happening, and was surprised.

"They're moving," she said. "They're alive!"

Julungul picked up her song-stick and began to beat the half-conscious sisters, breaking all their bones in the process. As soon as they were pulpy, she swallowed them down once more. Then she slithered back into the sacred waterhole.

Still Julungul could not erase from her mind what she had done. "Maybe those two women were my relatives, *dua* or *jiritja*," she thought. Again she rose up out of the waterhole and stood erect, spitting forth water and lightning. Again she fell back on the ground nearby, making a noise like thunder as she smashed the bones of the women inside her.

A snake from a far country inquired of Julungul, "Tell me now, what have you eaten?"

Julungul replied, "A kangaroo."

Another snake from a different country called out, "You haven't eaten kangaroo. You've eaten good food. Tell me the truth."

Finally Julungul admitted, "All right. I've eaten the Wauwalak Sisters."

The snake called back, "You're lucky. You've eaten two women. I've only eaten birds. Why don't you give me some?"

But Julungul was reluctant. "I can't," she said. "The Wauwalak Sisters are *maraiin*. Now they are my *maraiin*, my sacred knowledge."

A third snake from the Wessel Islands made a similar inquiry of Julungul: "Have you eaten blue-fish?"

"Yes," called Julungul.

"Ah," replied the snake from the Wessel Islands. "I heard thunder. You must have eaten good meat."

Julungul soon realized that it was not herself but the Wauwalak Sisters who were speaking. Their spirits were speaking out of her mouth. They were saying, "We're here now. We are inside the Snake. She has eaten us. Now we are *maraiin*, the sacred knowledge of Julungul. Our spirits talk through her for all those in another country."

Julungul returned to her camp at Muruwul. She said to all the snakes (including her husband) in the pool:

"Come on, all my sons and daughters. Join me in my shelter." Then she spoke as one with the voices of the Wauwalak Sisters inside her, "To you all I give my ceremonies."

Julungul could see the sun rising. She told her people to remain behind while she departed for a distant cave.

"I've given you the ceremonies," she said before she entered the cave. Then she placed a large boulder over the entrance so that no-one could come in or out.[1]

And so the myth ends. The Great Snake Julungul returns to the Dreaming after bestowing sacred ritual upon her people. The voice within her is the spirit of fecundity and dance, the sacred voice of birth and ceremony. The swallowing of the Mother of the World, the destined Bride of the Sun, by the Divine Snake clothed in all her reptilian integument of nonentity, echoes the Brhadaranyaka Upanishad where it says, 'Lead us from nonentity to being, darkness to light.' Until then the bride-elect in her guise as the Wauwalak Sisters was 'lying in the coils' of evil. Purified at last, Julungul is stripped of her reptilian aspects as dawn comes. All her adherent potentiality is put aside and she robes herself in 'sunny garments' in readiness for betrothal.

The death of the two women at the hands of Julungul is a felicity and consumption most to be desired. If the Divine Snake chooses to devour the Wauwalak Sisters, this is not merely a consumption but an incorporation. It represents both a 'rapture' and a 'transport' in every sense of these words. And inasmuch as it is Mother Earth, none other than the Vedic Eve (who was also beguiled by the Serpent) that is consumed, then we must recognize that all creation is feminine in God. The primordial snake really is the Godhead, as distinguished from the proceeding God — a protean being whose singular form is nonetheless the form of very different things. Julungul's bisexuality renders it a 'Supreme Identity' capable of transcending any limitations imposed by the concept of duality.

So we are at once moving into a region of universal symbolism. The sacrifice of the Wauwalak Sisters hints at a deep blood-bond with those protean forces which defy description, except at the level of mythogenesis. Only when we turn our attention to the Kunapipi songs do we begin to recognize a series of timeless motifs which spring from the Great Snake's heart. Where it says:

> Julungul crawls along, the tip of her tail twitching;
> As she slithers she speaks from her heart.
> Swallowing the Wauwalak, to the depths of her belly
> The mouth of her nest is blocked as she enters.

We know that her 'twitching tail' described here can also refer to her penis. The sexual overtones make us aware of how potent this act of consumption becomes. While Berndt stresses the sexual symbolism of the myth ('the Snake is a penis; the shelter a vulva') he does so, one feels, at the behest of Freudian interpretation then very much in vogue. Nonetheless one cannot ignore the powerful sexual imagery within the myth itself, nor the comments made by the initiates who often liken the events to the act of copulation. It is hoped that in the following chapters we will extend the meaning of the myth beyond that of sexual symbolism. The real talent of Aborigines is not to 'reduce' their myths to reflect a physical reality only, but to 'raise' them to the point where they embrace the supramundane realm of the Dreaming itself.

But before we do so, it is necessary to refer to the corpus of songs which accompany the rituals. Most of these songs are regarded as sacred: that is, they are actual songs sung by the Dreaming heroes at the time of the Dreaming. Their rhythm and content have stretched uninterrupted throughout the ages, and will continue to do so into the future. As one informant remarked to Berndt, 'These songs are the echo of those first sung by the Wauwalak Sisters and the Kunapipi people [Ancestors]. The spirit of this echo goes on forever. When we sing today, we take up the echo and make a sound [of our own].'[2] Once possessed by the Ancestral Beings, these songs give to the ritual not only a special 'atmosphere' but a sense of profound continuity and veracity. They have been passed down to humankind from the interworld of nature to be held in trust as the divine expression of the Dreaming heroes.

Of course they have not remained unaltered during this period of transition. Various songmen have transposed words, occasionally elaborated on certain themes, and re-arranged word-order to suit their purpose. Some have re-interpreted them in accordance with individual needs and cultural trends. In other cases modern motifs have crept in. But essentially there has been little change to the songs since they, too, are regarded as *maraiin* or sacred. Just as Euripides could justify his own work by the remark, 'The myth is not my own, I had it from my mother,' so too could the Aboriginal songmen argue that the Kunapipi songs came from a trans-human source.

As there are many songs that make up the corpus of Kunapipi ritual, a selection only will be detailed here in order to suggest their raw strength and power. The reader who wishes to explore them in more detail should refer to the work of Berndt already mentioned.

> Here is the Snake and its bullroarer;
> Hear it whirring as the young men's bodies are
> smeared with blood.
>
> Into the billabong a creek runs where the Snake lives,
> His bubbles rising to the surface of the billabong.
>
> Lightning strikes a tree near the *kanala* river;
> It burns there near the *kanala*, while the Snake drags

The Waulwalak Sisters

its balls behind.

The Snake throws earth afar as he digs, while the
Trickling stream washes down the Wauwalak's blood
In lumps. There's blood on the bullroarer's string.

They're swallowing slices of salty yam,
Removing its skin, roots and all.

The blue-tongued lizard squirms into its hole,
Broad-bodied, its backbone high-humped.

There is a fat buck wallaby standing by her mate
Who is arching her back, chewing on sweet grass.

Julungul crawls along, the tip of her tail twitching;
As she slithers she speaks from the heart.

Swallowing the Wauwalak, to the depths of her belly,
The mouth of her nest is blocked as she enters.

Talking to herself, she slithers along, while
On the ground pools of urine lie in her wake.

The Snake blinks as she crawls along, her body
Writhing from what she has eaten.

Pandanus branches quiver in pouring rain, and
New green shoots tremble as the trunk sways.

There is a blanket lizard, his body poised
As he watches the rain-water swirling past.

In the shallow waters of Muruwul billabong
A shag is fishing among the paperbark trees.

In step the Kandjarlkala Spirits walk along
Singing as they quit the jungle. They see

Giant anthills and a *djiragit* bird,
Its wings fluttering quickly as it flies.

The Waulwalak Sisters

The Spirits paint their bodies with coloured clay
Washed down from the steep face of cliffs.

A wallaby watches them from a boulder
Then it hops away, over a ridge.

In the water a black snake swims, her eggs
Inside her body like seeds in a fig.

There is a mangrove fish with its young,
Fluttering its fins and tail.

Its nose floating on the surface, a crocodile
Swims quietly along, shifting its tail.

Bark falls from an apricot tree into the water...

And the women make love, their clitori
Stimulated by the rubbing action of penes.

Bandicoots are at play, possums too are dancing,
While a jungle fowl cries out as it flies away.

Ah! The beauty of a young girl's breasts
And her mount of Venus, musky with love.

So shy is she, her pubic hair stiff
With old love and man-juices.

All of them are wearing headbands
While they dance the Kunapipi dance.

At Muruwul the snake splits trees,
The noise of lightning rolling from her belly.

On an upper branch an owl sits and blinks, while
Men with cut penises talk among themselves.

The Spirits emerge from the jungle, see
The morning pigeon, water on the ground.

Pissing on the ground, their balls hanging,

The Waulwalak Sisters

The men jerk their penises before the women.

A small snake lies there, its belly full
And tail twitching, twitching...

A crane stands on a sandbank with its young
Watching, watching for fish...

Geese fly above the swamplands,
A canoe's prow slowly skims the water...

Arm blood spurts forth as brother daubs brother...

Hear the sound of the green-backed turtle
As it swims near the edge of the bank!

See the spiked spear-head, its shaft bulky with wax...

A shy young girl shrugs her shoulders,
Throws back her hair and extends her breasts
As she sidles towards a new act of love.

Oh! The Wauwalak is carrying her baby
Under her arm as it begins to cry.

The two sisters walk along, carrying
Their baby, they walk along...

A sweet smell of love-juices, before loving
Linger in the air at the end of the dance.

Her arm-band loose, her skin soft like fur;
Shyly she walks back to her husband, where
They laugh at her love-making with another man

She removes her pubic cloth, opens wide
Her legs so that he might lie with her.

They make love, child-driven
The spear-thrower there with its hook,
Fire and ashes filling the air with sparks.

The Waulwalak Sisters

Men with red, black and white loincloths
Sit there, smoking their long pipes,

Their cut penises ejaculating, ejaculating
Semen as white as mist.

The Snake shits as it crawls around Muruwul...

Wirlkul's nipples rise up and she smells of
love-juices...

Crocodiles nest on the banks of the creek
As mist covers the surface...

This is a much-condensed version of a cycle of songs known as the *kudjiga*, a word which implies their 'inside' or esoteric character. At first reading perhaps, the general images from nature, along with its highly charged sexual interpolations, suggest two different themes at work. That is, until one realizes that these songs are adjuncts to the myth itself. The ritual participants know the myth by heart, so as far as they are concerned these songs merely provide a poetic dimension to the rites. Nature is one of the essential 'players' in the enactment. It looks on, observes, and by its actions sometimes 'comments' on the confrontation between the Wauwalak Sisters and Julungul. The primary images of female fecundity, incest, water, phallus and snake, lightning and rain, warn us, however, that we are in the presence of a myth whose erotic elements suggest more than the cessation of sexual taboos during the course of the ceremony. For the Aborigines, their enactment of the Kunapipi rites brings them in contact with the principial order of Creation: sexual licence is but a preamble to that encounter. What they are doing is re-creating that pristine moment when the World and all its cultural forms were first conceived. Attempting to 'shake off' the serpent is itself proof of Mother Earth's original orphidian nature; she, like the snake, is footless. Just as Agni's Mother (Rg Veda III.55.14) is described as one who 'stands erect', so too does Julungul at the moment when she rises from her waterhole.

84

In this sense the Great Snake becomes an embodiment of the 'Serpent Queen' who is the principle and source of all nourishment.

We are ready to embark upon a more detailed analysis of the Wauwalak myth now that we are in possession of most of the key elements. Though we cannot sit in the firelight and watch the dancers, nor can we hear the rhythm of clap-stick or the baleful droning of didgeridoo, we can at least imagine the sacred ground of *nongaru*. Before us lies the clearing: a crescent-shaped trench about twelve feet long has been dug out, at once symbol of Julungul's track as she fell after swallowing the sisters, as well as their crouching position in the shelter before the Snake swallowed them. Its esoteric meaning reflects the uterus of the older Wauwalak Sister, Gungman. Kunapipi, the Old Woman, is said to be invisibly present in this trench, and her life-giving powers are ready to flow forth in company with the sexual actions of the dancers. All the totemic beings are present: possum, bandicoot, snakes, birds and fish. The stage is set. The principial division between *dua* and *jiritja* underlies a far-reaching destiny for all humankind — that of making the 'Many into One' again. We, too, stand at the very threshold of this ancient rite, awaiting a visitation from the Great Snake as she slowly squirms her way up out of the Hole of Life to visit us in our uterine shelter.

CHAPTER 7
Muruwul Waterhole

At the beginning of the myth we are confronted by the
Wauwalak Sisters, symbols of order and foreknowledge. They
are the paths of 'day and night' and their journey away from
their principial homeland is in keeping with the sundering of the
'One into Many' at the time of Creation. Their land, the *dua*
land, has not yet experienced such a hiatus or fragmentation
before, although this is in keeping with its desire to become
manifest. It is a protean realm where unity reigns. The incestuous
relationship between the elder sister, Gungman, with one of her
clansmen, however, signals a 'fall' from grace. Multiplicity now
exists. The fecundation of the maternal darkness within an
incest relationship from which a new child is to be born is a
powerful symbol of 'light (the son) illuminating (inseminating)
darkness' (the mother). As Christ was the bridegroom of Mary
(i.e. Mother Church), so too does Gungman bear her own
clansman's child whose birth announces the reign of duality in
the form of the *dua* and *jiritja* moieties. So that out of unity
multiplicity is born. Gungman bears within her the male by
which she is begotten. According to Sir George Ripley, a
seventeenth-century alchemist, the mother-son, sister-brother
incest was designed to make the land more fruitful again.[1]
Furthermore the cultural lineaments which determine the way
both family and tribal structures work in the world have also
been born. Men and women can now be 'one or the other', and
so the underlying principle of cosmic order on the plane of
manifestation is initiated. The 'pairs of opposites' that were
encountered in Part I are once more brought into play. The
Wauwalak Sisters may also be identified with the frog-women
whom Ankotarinja attacked at Parr Erultja.

The two women journey in the direction of Muruwul, the
sacred waters, naming all the animals along the way. Here the

uroboric male-female anonymity before Creation is affirmed by the waterhole where the Divine Snake lives. We know that the 'primordial ocean' is characterized by a uroboric snake encompassing the earth born of it. This snake, according to Egyptian belief, desires to 'destroy everything I have created. The earth will again appear as a primordial ocean, as endless as in the beginning. I, then, am everything that remains... after I have turned myself back into a snake that *no man knows*' (our italics).[2] Julungul's invisible presence is waiting there to destroy all, to revoke the passage towards multiplicity as it is invested in the Wauwalak Sisters, and so invoke the paradoxical desire of manifestation to return to its origin, to a state of unity. But this cannot be, since the Wauwalak Sisters 'name' animals and birds — that is, they bring them into being through the use of language, the Divine Word. The movement towards consciousness is therefore confirmed: in differentiation we see the beauty of the manifested world made intrinsic for the first time. For all her protean strength Julungul remains asleep in her pool while the sisters continue to invoke the world.

We are aware, too, that these women bear with them the rudiments of culture: spears, feathered string and cane armlets and head-bands. One of them wears a girdle. They have brought with them into the world those things required to live as beings who are more than just animals. These women are culture-bearers. The spiritual heritage of the Dreaming rests in their dillybags, along with all the animals they have created for food. Matriarchal and world-ordering, they enter the sphere of manifestation with a vigour that defies that of Julungul, at least initially. The Great Snake, on the other hand, according to Vedic doctrine at least, is the 'impotent godhead', 'blind, halt and ineffectual' who can only 'extend himself, assuming forms', as she slumbers in the deep recesses of the waterhole. More importantly perhaps, the sisters are conscious of their power of pro-creation. Is it not they who suggest that whatever they name and catch shall be *maraiin* (sacred) in due time? So they carry into the world the concepts of sacred law, ritual, indeed all those forms needed to render in metaphor the moment of Creation — dance and song among them. The Wauwalak Sisters are not so much victims of primordial incest as it might first appear to be, but are instead the divinely appointed bearers of all metaphysical knowledge on earth. In their dillybags they carry all the secrets of life, much as if these were their own wombs.

We have seen that Gungman bears within her body multiplicity in the form of the child born into the *jiritja* moiety. This child carries the stamp of division on its brow. The lingering wound that accompanies its birth, the blood-spore on the ground, these are none other than a prefigurement of the sacrifice which accompanies all manifestation, all duality, all intimations of good and evil. The child, though female, represents the sun, since in Aboriginal cosmology the first-appearing sun is both female and ophidic.[3] Gungman, in her guise as the Great Mother (Kunapipi), gives birth to the sun which stands at the centre of all matriarchal mysteries. We see the daughter standing behind the Mother Goddess in Akkadian reliefs with tendrils sprouting from her body. These symbolize the tree or earth. Gungman's daughter is an archetype for the birth of the Divine Child. She is Horus, Osiris, Dionysus and Christ in their feminine-solar aspect.

So the Wauwalak Sisters arrive at Muruwul waterhole, home of the Serpent. We know that as a mother Gungman stands for the foundation of social life and hence of human culture. The blood mystery of birth imposes its own hierarchy of values upon the surrounding wilderness. She 'desecrates' the place with her birth-blood, so bringing about a nexus between the sacred and the profane. Until then these conditions had remained apart. Furthermore the Great Snake so far has been immune from all contact with the world. When the animals in Gungman's dilly-bag are 'sacrificed' on the fire, they rise up again, revivified by their encounter with light and fire. As Christ says, 'He that is near me is near the fire' and 'Cleave the wood and I am there.'[4] Hence these animals 'cleaved the wood' and hurried into the sacred waterhole to be near the fire. This event had already been prefigured when the Wauwalak Sisters had remarked on the fact that the animals would become *maraiin* later. Their sacerdotal nature was intrinsic to their being, as they chose to 'return' to their maker, Julungul.

The sacred waterhole is an important motif in Aboriginal cosmology and belief. Throughout Australia there are countless pools dedicated to the memory of the Rainbow Serpent. This is nature's *temenos*, its holy ground. No man can approach such a place without being conscious of its implications. To be in the invisible presence of the Great Snake is to be aware of the existence of a timeless numinous reality. According to Greek mythology the Great Snake in the form of Cronos bore the cosmic egg containing the entire cosmos.[5] In an Orphic hymn his offspring Zeus is spoken of as the 'foundation of the earth and starry heavens' as well as being 'male and divine virgin'.[6] He is closely associated with lightning, the sun and the moon just as Julungul is. In Julungul we have the prototype of all orphidic figures, the snake that embodies both feminine and masculine traits. While Julungul is referred to as 'she' throughout the myth, we are conscious that 'she' is also 'he'.

Muruwul represents the primordial pool of being. Into this all nature ultimately returns. It was no accident that the Wauwalak Sisters found themselves camped by the sacred waterhole since it was acknowledged as their destination at the commencement of the myth. They knew where they were going. The sisters had 'named' all creatures on their way there, after all, and had then presided over the animals' return to the empyrian. In the act of desecrating the pool, death and rebirth is implicitly acknowledged. The blood of life flows back into the sacred waters, stimulating a new birth by way of the awakening movements of Julungul. The Great Snake shrugs off its primordial slumber. While there is some suggestion that Gungman's blood pollutes the waterhole, we also know that Aborigines consider menstruation *maraiin* or sacred. Therefore the snake's interest in the blood-spore implies divine interest rather than rejection.

During the Kunapipi ceremony a number of head-men are

said to cut a vein inside their elbow and allow the blood to flow in imitation of the menstrual and afterbirth blood-flow of the Wauwalak Sisters. While at one level this incisure may be a substitute for sub-incision of the penis, it is clearly recognized by the participants as being also an act of identifying with 'Mother Kunapipi' and the bleeding of the 'Spring' women at the beginning of their menstrual cycle. The men do not regard the blood-flow into the sacred waterhole as a desecration so much as an embodiment of the flow of eternal life within themselves. 'Ah, very good,' they say. 'That is the blood of the Spring Women [in me]'.[7] Furthermore, the 'shout' of Julungul as he smells the blood is duplicated by a bullroarer made from a clean piece of wood cut from the tree which Julungul had split with lightning. The coming-together of the blood of the Wauwalak Sisters and the cry of the Serpent echo a *coniunctio* between *nous* and *physis*, soul and body. The Wauwalak Sisters and Julungul, therefore, represent a 'pair of opposites' struggling to free itself of its inherent centrifugence. In their confrontation one perceives the emergence of a duplex, a *utriusque capex* ('capable of both').

The sound of the bullroarer announces the rumblings of Julungul as it awakes. According to the participants the sound is a 'little bit low', spasmodic and quick, for this snake is full from having eaten so many young men at the *nongaru* ground during the age-grading rituals. We now know that Julungul has smelt the blood of birth, and as a result her curiosity is aroused. She has raised her head above the water, her nostrils quivering as she sprays water into the air to form rainclouds. Linking the Great Snake with the advent of the wet season reinforces the idea that the Wauwalak Sisters, in spite of their fecundity, are essentially barren, since they represent the dry season before the beginning of the monsoon. Warner[8] argues that the weather symbolism surrounding the snake-swallowing-the-women signifies the 'swallowing of the earth by the rainy season.' The rainy season literally 'engulfs' the dry season as men 'possess' women, or that the initiated 'swallow up' the uninitiated as famine destroys plenty. Levi-Strauss maintains that such homologies are said to achieve the unification of heterogeneous semantic fields. These account for nature's varied activities in the form of scarcity of food due to the sterility of the land in the dry season, as well as its converse. But such interpretations do not take into account the full metaphysical implications of the myth, as they are at pains to reduce Aboriginal thinking to material correlations only. There is no doubt that the actions of nature are implied in all mythic events; however, to say as Roheim does that the main function of the Kunapipi myth is to satisfy in fantasy the 'wish for reunion with the mother' while endeavouring to achieve a 'deflection of libido away from the mother onto the father', or that it typifies 'fantasies and anxieties connected with vagina and uterus', serves little but to denigrate all mythic activity.[9] We are not dealing here with primitive fantasies but with the prototypical explanation of all metaphysical phenomena.[10]

Nonetheless, the formation of rainclouds signals the essentially fructive nature of Julungul's intentions. The Great Snake has interpreted the blood-spore of Gungman as a heraldic gesture of fecundity and abundance of which she is exemplar. Rain is the fertilizing principle *par excellence.* Julungul's emergence from the waters echoes the passage of the rainbow across the sky, so creating the 'Bridge of the Spirit' joining the material to the spiritual world. As St Gregory remarks, 'If "clouds" are holy preachers, the rains from the clouds are the words of their preaching'. To Swedenborg, 'Rain signifies divine truth from heaven.' As the Rainbow Serpent, Julungul is linked to the image of the ladder and the spiritual aspirations it represents. She is yearning to climb higher, to spread her beneficence over all. The deluge mentioned in the myth means much more than the end of the dry season precipitated by Gungman's continual bleeding. Her bleeding, in fact, is a signal for Julungul to emerge from her primordial sleep and enter the world. Giving birth to a *jiritja* being, and so precipitating duality in the world, has led to a situation whereby the divine principle (in the form of the Dreaming hero, Julungul) must enter the world also. From the divine obscurity of Muruwul waterhole Julungul comes forth,

PLATE 1

Ankotarinja is seen wearing the tjuruna *on his head which he wore as he emerged from the ground at the moment of world-birth. The two men are wearing the body-paintings central to the rituals. Bullroarers are seen hanging from their decorations. The head-dress represents the towering* tnatantja *that sprang from the head of the original ancestor.*

PLATE 2

Here Ankotarinja bears the great tjuruna talkau *on his head. This object fell from his head when his heart burned with anger against the* tilpa *men at Parr Erultja.*

PLATE 3
In number three, Ankotarinja is seen with a simple headgear -
devoid of all bullroarers - which were left behind while en route to
Parr Erultja.
In number four, Ankotarinja is seen as he arrived at Par Erultja.

PLATE 4
A frieze of Wanjina figures in a cave near Mount Barnett in the central Kimberley region. Note the bones of the deceased at the foot of the photograph.

PLATE 5
Churinga *custodians seated beside recently returned* churinga.
Behind them note the churinga *store-house made up of a platform
built in a tree. These* churinga *are similar to those once located at
Parr Erultja. Each board embodies the spiritual essence of a
totemic hero.*

PLATE 6
The man on the right is wearing a sacred tnatantja *pole on his head. This is the kind of pole that Ankotarinja discovered protruding from his head at Ankota.*

PLATE 7
The sacred tnatantja *pole as depicted in the kangaroo totemic
ceremony of the Aranda people. As the Cosmic Tree, it serves to
situate the world, and humankind, between the two realms - that
of the material and the metaphysical.*

PLATE 8
Another version of the tnatantja *used during a rain-dance.*

The photographs are by courtesy of Mitchell Library and Oceania Publications.
The cover photograph is by courtesy of Colin Beard.

utterly blind to her own subject. So unequivocally is she herself that the Great Snake can only emanate as rain and lightning. Her actions echo that of Ibn Arabi's remark, 'I was a hidden treasure desiring to be known.' Julungul finally emerged from what Ibn Arabi called the 'carpet' (unknowable essence) by way of rain manifesting itself on the phenomenal world.[11] Julungul too wishes to be known.

This action on the part of Julungul, far from being that of a deity in a state of anger at the desecration of her haven, is rather the divine act of an avatar coming-into-being. Julungul, the Rainbow Serpent, has emerged from its subluminary realm beneath the waters. She has rained forth her presence, and 'spoken from the heart' as she presides over 'new green shoots' which tremble in their succulence. Julungul's method of expression is sublime action; how she does so only *appears* to be negative in the light of mythic narrative. What we are observing here is the deliberate veiling of the essential nature of all her activity. To the young novice, lying on the *nongaru* ground immersed in his own ignorance, Julungul's behaviour seems maleficent, and therefore deliberately designed to provoke fear and trembling. Her attack on the Wauwalak Sisters implies a wish to destroy the human condition, whereas the contrary is nearer the truth. The heavy downpour signals the need for all humankind to retreat into the 'shelter' of meditation in order to understand the significance of the Great Snake's actions. Rain brings on new growth, a regeneration after a relatively fallow period of naming things in the world. The novice must learn how to understand, must begin to see the world as more than a mere reflection of his individual identity. Along with the Wauwalak Sisters he must enter the haven of deeper knowledge if he is to become a fully rounded warrior, father and ritual participant. He must learn to accept the Great Snake as the 'ruler of the land in which he dwells'.

It is at this point in the narrative that Julungul begins to manifest more masculine traits. Neumann states that in contrast to the feminine mysteries, the transformation mysteries of the

Archetypal Masculine have the character of a surprise attack, and sudden eruptions are said to be the decisive factor. Lightning is the characteristic symbol of these.[12] Thus we see a corresponding movement away from the symbolically feminine underworld as it is realized in the waterhole. The Great Snake is beginning to emerge from its primordial bisexual aspect to become a more seminal, vivifying force. He has become like Heracles, etymologically the 'coiled serpent' and descendent of Cronus, the serpent-god and god of time. His lightning is different from natural lightning because it partakes of all the numinous qualities of deity. The symbol of the serpent as an important symbol of deity finds a later expression in St John's (3:14) dictum, 'And as Moses lifted up the serpent in the wilderness, even so must the Son of Man be lifted up.' Christ is seen as a sapiential serpent in subsequent Christian symbolism. Thunder and lightning presage at the birth of a significant avatar. Julungul has entered the world.

The Wauwalak Sisters do not become aware of this event as anything other than a natural one. They cannot see beyond conventional forms. It is only when Julungul drags himself towards them that they begin to identify him as an embodiment of sacrifice and regeneration. The ambitious, some might say life-giving and death-dealing fascination of the Great Snake (i.e. she represents the belly of the 'Old Woman' or Earth Goddess herself) hypnotises them. They feel powerless before her advance. Only by retreating into the shelter, the cosmic egg, are they able to feel safe from her clutches. But this is an illusion: Julungul in her capacity as the 'dragon that invests the rivers' (Rg Veda I. 52. 2) is ready to crush them in her coils. She is ready to take up the cosmic egg in which they huddle, and draw it into herself. She becomes the uroborus, the celestial serpent that coils around the 'glittering starry heaven',[13] her tail in her mouth. Julungul takes on the garb of the sun as she traverses the firmament. She desires to enter the shelter where the two women huddle just as the sun penetrates and so inseminates the earth with its life-giving warmth. The earlier reliance on sexual symbolism by

Berndt is now given an added dimension in the light of this collusion between sun and snake. The solar serpent is about to enter the cosmic egg and fertilize it in accordance with its stellar role. It is said that the sun often appears as a serpent accompanied by seven planets. The disc of the sun was also seen as a 'great dragon with its tail in its mouth.'[14]

So far we have encountered a number of important motifs while accompanying the Wauwalak Sisters to Muruwul waterhole. Incest, birth, the naming of animals and the awakening of the Great Snake from her primordial slumber — that is, her undifferentiated state — these, along with others, have begun to emerge as significant carriers of metaphysical import. What at first seemed like an arbitrary journey across an unnamed landscape at the time of the Dreaming has now taken on a more intrinsic aspect. Like Ankotarinja's emergence from the creekbed at Ankota, the drama of the Wauwalak Sisters and their escape from incestuous clansmen has left us with a feeling that we are about to confront a *hieros gamos*, or sacred marriage, between the spirit and the earth. Ritual coition is about to be enacted between the Wauwalak Sisters huddled in their shelter and the transcendent phallus, namely Julungul. All the ritual elements of this marriage have been played out: the receptive *yoni* has been constructed by the women to await the bridegroom. Their tiny shelter made of bark on the edge of Muruwul becomes the *cista mystica* — that is, the 'mystic box' wherein the ritual vessel of rebirth is housed. According to the Gnostics, such a chest was only brought forth at the hour of their mysteries. In their doctrine the meaning of the serpent and his encounter with the shelter is fully revealed:

> The cosmos consists of Father, Son and Matter. Each of these three principles contain infinitely many forces. Midway between the Father and Matter, the Son, the Logos, has his place, the Serpent that moves eternally towards the unmoved Father and moved Matter; now it turns to the Father and gathers up forces in its countenance; and now, after receiving the forces, it turns towards Matter, and upon Matter, which is without attribute and

form, the Son imprints the ideas which have previously been
imprinted upon the Son by the Father.

Now no one can be saved and rise up again without the Son, who
is the serpent. For it is he who brought the paternal models down
from above, and it is he who carries back again those who have been
awakened from sleep and have reassumed the features of the
Father.[15]

While it should be understood that the above text reflects an
interesting parallel to the Wauwalak material, it should not be
taken as fact that Aboriginal cosmology had evolved such
complex models of theological expression. Julungul is not a
Gnostic serpent; rather he is an ancient forerunner of his
Gnostic cousin, Nahash. It is evident from what has already been
said that Julungul occupies the interworld 'midway between
Father and Matter' in the same way as Nahash. All Julungul's
actions suggest that she receives her powers from the interworld
of nature which she passes onto the world of matter. The
prototypal nature of all Julungul's actions places her in the
category of an avatar. She does indeed imprint certain ideas
upon matter — ideas which stem from the Dreaming itself. The
Wauwalak myth gives us further insight into the profound
workings of mythogenesis. Snake, virgin, solar birth, celestial
waters and sacred womb rise up as archetypes to fuel our
imagination. As this happens we find ourselves transported
back into the dim reaches of collective memory where the origin
of all *mythos* resides as a snake coiled around the cosmic egg of
world-birth, indeed the very concept of belief itself.

CHAPTER 8
Swallowing the Women

It is said that in the night of Brahma nature is inert, and cannot dance until Shiva wills it. But when Shiva rises from His rapture, the act of dancing sends through inert matter waves of awakening sound. Matter begins also to dance, appearing as a glorious chorus about Him. In dancing, Shiva is able to sustain matter's manifold and evolving phenomena. In the fullness of time, and still dancing, Shiva destroys all forms and names by fire, thus preparing the ground for renewal. The god dances to maintain the life of the cosmos and to give release to those who seek Him. The dance signifies rhythmic play as the source of all movement within the cosmos. Its secondary purpose is to release the countless souls of men from the snare of illusion. According to Vedic sources the place of the dance (*Chidambaram*) represents the Centre of the Universe within the Heart.[1]

The action of the Wauwalak Sisters in the face of Julungul's advance are a significant turning-point in the relationship between soul and matter. It would be wrong to suggest that the most profound interpretation of the Wauwalak Sisters' dance is present in the minds of those Aborigines who celebrate it today; but it has to be said that the dance itself is its own clearest image of the *activity* of the Dreaming spirits, whether men understand its symbolism or not. One must acknowledge that the esoteric elements of the dance are not readily approachable except by way of comparison and allusion. It appears that the Wauwalak Sisters dance to defend themselves. In reality they are dancing in the spirit of Eros, 'that ancient one' according to Lucian, whose 'primal dancing clearly set forth in the choral dance of the constellations, and in the planets and fixed stars, their interweaving and interchange and orderly harmony.' Wirlkul's swaying body represents much more than erotic display: she is invoking celestial harmonies which both beguile and arrest

Julungul (i.e. the sun) in her course.

In the snake dance we have the precursor of all mystic dances. According to ancient sources the dance stands at the beginning of all things. It lies at the origin of all physical activity just as the pulsation at the heart of all sub-atomic activity prefigures matter's realization on the plane of *physis*. The Wauwalak Sisters are clearly engaged in a cosmic dance. Their simple actions (shuffling feet, swaying the body, and moving gracefully) are the prototype of all ritual gestures, the *mudras* which pervade the social sphere and affirm the sanctity of the Present. Like words, these gestures are the expressions of support and spiritual resolve. The women dance in front of their shelter, inviting the Great Snake to possess them even as they call out to him to 'Go away!' This gesture is like that of the *yoni mudra*, implying the presence and availability of the female organ to the Tantric adept, which in turn signifies the proximity of an altar. The bark shelter becomes the embodiment of the sacred *yoni* in the Kunapipi myth, the principial altar upon which matter is sacrificed in the interest of celestial harmony. Julungul is the incarnation of the high priest who presides over the sacrificial offering.[2]

The Wauwalak Sisters attempt to enchant Julungul outside the entrance to their shelter, alternately protecting themselves and the child within. This is no ordinary dance designed merely to seduce the serpent. It is a cosmic dance which presides over the earth's quickening, over the realization of what appears in the world, of the process whereby all that has previously been in the belly of the sleeping serpent now exists on the plane of manifestation. Wirlkul weaves cats'-cradles with her fingers, transforming the air into a series of intricate designs which appear and disappear as soon as they are contrived. She builds 'castles in the air', and weaves a net of fantasy before Julungul's eyes. The ancient Egyptians also believed in the existence of a net in the Underworld which the deceased was required to avoid if he wished to rise from the dead.[3] Such a net was said to symbolise a certain condition of the inner nature which shut the man into the limitations of the conventional life of the world, and shut him off from the memory of his true self. According to the Upanishads (Svetasvatara Upanishad, V), one deity 'spreads out his net in many modes for everyone in this field of illusion, and draws it in again.' Wirlkul spreads her nets before the eyes of Julungul in the same way, presenting her with an image of illusion which momentarily arrests her in his track. Julungul is repeatedly confronted with a cosmic dancer who wants to draw her into the world, to make her a part of the process of materialization. In the act of being seduced she is turning away from the Father towards Matter. She is being made a world-creator even as her immediate object is to attack those who have desecrated the sanctity of her waterhole.

A more prosaic explanation of these events can be accepted also. According to Aboriginal belief the act of polluting the well provoked Julungul into spitting into the sky and causing rain by hissing. This act produced a black cloud and a torrential downpour. The Aborigines say that the Great Snake is responsible for the northwest monsoon. Thunder is her voice, lightning her forked tongue, rain her saliva and the rainbow a manifestation of her presence. One informant said: 'Those two women tried to stop the rain because the water came like a flood and tried to cover them all up. That is all the same as the snake swallowing them. The women tried to stop the snake because he was the flood and the wet season covering the earth.'[4]

Here there is a parallel with the myth of Persephone and the dances performed in the Graeco-Kore cults. Persephone's abduction by Hades who carries her off into the Underworld is expressed in a dance in which a piece of rope is held by the dancers. It is suggested by Kerényi that the dance reflects the fable of Ariadne and her desire to aid in the escape of her lover from the Labyrinth (i.e. from the Underworld).[5] The rope/net/cats'-cradle motif reflects the proximity of the Underworld, of death, and the desire to return from it. The Wauwalak Sisters wish to draw attention to the unending torrent of ephemeral forms, ever tangibly present, yet nonetheless divinely ordered.

Nature, it seems, is now taking shelter in the very maelstrom of the world.

The relationship between the labyrinth and the death-and-rebirth motif is normally associated with the entrance to a cave or constructed dwelling. According to Layard,[6] the person who presides over it is normally a woman. Whether the labyrinth takes on the infinitely confusing lines (i.e. the net or cats'-cradle) or the shape of the 'guardian spirit' herself, or whether it becomes the way by which the soul of the deceased is able to pass through the intricate devouring labyrinth, in each case we have before us the conception of the divine body as the road travelled by itself and its seeker.[7] The labyrinthine way becomes the descent of the male as it follows the sun into the devouring underworld, into the deathly womb of the Terrible Mother. Julungul inches towards the guardian spirit who is none other than Wirlkul and Gungman as they dance before the entrance to the Underworld.

It is a moment to savour. The initiatory moment when the young men of the tribe choose to identify with the Divine Feminine in the personage of the Wauwalak Sisters means that they will be devoured by the Great Snake. They must cross over into the Underworld and return as adults. The Wauwalak Sisters are inviting them to become a part of their realm, and begin to acknowledge how the feminine principle was the original custodian of law and custom. Berndt argues that the myth hides a significant primordial event: the stealing of this knowledge by the men from the women. All the ritual actions are designed to cover up this theft, and so invest men with their patrilineal authority. This may be so; but it only goes half way to exploring the cosmic nature of the dance and the seduction of the serpent. The essential significance of this metaphor is in the way it underlies the materialization of the universe, and affirms the importance of the 'pair of opposites' — namely, death-and-rebirth.

Gungman cries out in despair, 'I am bleeding!' The Snake draws closer. She acknowledges at once that her menstruation is regarded as dangerous and baleful, and that she should be secluded from the rays of sun and moon. Since light is the progenitive power, she must not beget at this time. She has become an incarnation of the Loathly Bride and thus conjoined with the serpent.[8] Her seclusion represents a temporary return to the primordial state, which is not, so to speak, human, but uncanny. Her menstruation is a kind of infection or possession; the subsequent purification followed by intercourse is the regeneration of her humanity, and a repetition of the nuptial rite by which she was first made a woman who had once been a nymph. The ancient marriage formula is echoed: 'I am Sky, you are Earth, I the Chant, you the Verses, let us be one, and bring forth offspring.' In the end, even Wirlkul begins to menstruate after her excessive exertions caused by her constant dancing, so that finally both women are conjoined with the serpent.

Lightning flashes. The delight in tasting ideal beauty is on the tip of Julungul's tongue. Though devoid of contact with intelligible things, such a prospect is in the intellectual-ecstatic order of being, transcendental, indivisible and self-manifested. This vision of beauty is an act of pure contemplation whereby Julungul begins to identify with the object of contemplation. Hers becomes the perfection of aesthetic contemplation which as 'very Self surveys the variegated world-picture as nothing other than the Self depicted on the mighty canvas of the Self, and takes a great delight therein' (Svatma-Nirupana 95). Traditionally a flash of lightning reflects the pure act of revelation wherein the deep silence, the quiddity of knowledge pertaining to the essence of Deity becomes known. In Indian iconography lightning is commonly represented in the form of golden snakes. The lightning emanating from Julungul can only be a symbol of her ophidian godhead, her supreme likeness of nature. As a 'snake without end', as a circle superimposed on a circle, the Great Snake proceeds from snakehood to snakehood by transforming her potentiality into act. As a streak of serpentine lightning the wayfarer returns to the source from which he came forth. 'The Person seen in the Lightning — I am He, and I indeed

101

am He' (Chandoga Upanishad IV.13.1). This image is further highlighted when Julungul coils around the shelter and puts her head inside. The uroborus, or snake biting its own tail, becomes a representation of the Godhead, the Father, and of Eternity.[9]

The moment when Julungul does so signals the climax of the myth. We are at once alerted to its sacramental sexual connotations. The shelter into which the Wauwalak Sisters retreat becomes the womb of all existences, none other than the Brahma-womb according to Vedic sources. Julungul is about to enter the womb of transcendent nature whose 'nature is my own, and when I resort to her, I pour forth at her with this whole body of being that has no independent will,' (Bhagavad Gita IX). As Eckhart remarks, 'From the Father's embrace of his own nature comes the eternal playing.' In the act of entering the shelter the Great Snake becomes a child-bearer in conformity with his/her Solar ancestry. She lays the embryo in the womb of nature. She impregnates the ground of all existence with the mystic substance of her Word — namely, the substance known as *ngeiakngeiakma*, the saliva of pro-generation. (The word *ngal*, often used for this salival substance, is associated with the ejaculation of semen. Ritual actors are painted white with a symbolic substance called *ngal*, signifying Julungul's saliva or semen.)

Regarded as the hieroglyph of eternity the uroborus can therefore say of himself, 'I am One and at the same time Many in myself' and so confirm his capacity to unite opposites. Drawn towards matter by the actions of the Wauwalak Sisters, Julungul is able to resolve this tension caused by a reversion to that of the hylic dimension when she literally consumes the principial cause of the diremption. In the ritual, uninitiated youths are said to be consumed by a supernatural being. The novices are regarded as having returned to the primordial uterus from which, through the good offices of the men, they are able to return safely, though with altered status.[10] In one cult variation blood-covered novices are seen to return to their mothers from between the legs of the initiated men. The rebirth of the boys as initiates is often associated with natural parturition. The act of being swallowed by the monster represents a dying; descent into the belly also signifies return to the embryonic state.[11] On the plane of the individual it represents the symbolism of death-and-rebirth. At the cosmological level the darkness of the monster's interior corresponds to the Chaos before the Creation. More than one layer of symbolism is being dealt with here: that of death, namely the conclusion of temporal existence, and consequently of the end of time, and the symbolism of return to the germinal mode of being, which precedes all forms and every temporal existence.[12]

It is a moment of extreme significance. Julungul opens his mouth and swallows first the child and then the sisters. Virgin, mother and child return to the primordial darkness of being. They who have precipitated the birth of multiplicity (in the form of the *dua/jiritja* moieties) have themselves been transformed into One again. Their digestion reduces them to essence, to what is classified as *maraiin* or sacred. Like the animals which they caught in the early part of the myth, they too have been transformed into spiritual substance. The Great Snake has taken back into itself all that partakes of multiplicity – and by implication, death itself. The act of swallowing the women and child, said to represent the act of coitus, may also symbolize the return of the Wauwalak Sisters to the womb of the Divine Mother, Kunapipi.[13] Thus the uroboric cycle is completed: the young men on the *nongaru* ground find themselves performing a rite of passage by returning to the mother-earth that made them. Such a rite is reiterated in numerous cultures throughout the world where a monster is said to swallow the neophytes, prior to their return to the world as initiates.[14]

Returning to Muruwul waterhole, we see Julungul stand erect in the air, a phallic-shaped body who, in one variation of the Kunapipi myth, is said to affirm the primacy of the *dua moiety* over all others as she surveys the world from her great height. "What is your language?" she is asked by other snakes in distant parts of Arnhem Land. To each inquiry she states that her language is that of her primal *dua* moiety, while they in turn affirm their allegiance to different (i.e. *jiritja*) languages of their own. "Ah, what a lot of languages we talk," she observes. Collectively she affirms that they all share the same sacred objects, and the same ceremonies. All men are intrinsically one, in spite of any differences that might be attributed to language. Superficially men might find themselves separated by words, although true brotherhood is recognized by the use of ritual objects and ceremonies held in common. From her Olympian height Julungul is able to see the differentiation of peoples in terms of place and language, yet she is also cognizant with their essential unity. In consuming the Wauwalak Sisters Julungul acknowledges that her body is the origin of all secret knowledge pertaining to the enigma of life, and the subsequent articulation of it. She is the source of all words which in themselves are the building-blocks that go to make up all new concepts and beliefs. She holds the key to *understanding*, to the sacred edifice of sapiential knowledge. Her verticality celebrates the contiguity between death and rebirth, between language and expression, between the power of words and the need to delineate culture.

Julungul's desire to explore the realm of language finds its parallel in the figure of Hermes, whose stone monument, the *herma*, is the stone from which the name of God stems. Phonetically *herma* corresponds to the Latin *sermo*, 'speech' or any verbal 'exposition.' It also finds its basic verbal root in *hermeneia*, 'explanation' or *hermeneus*, 'interpreter', which makes him a linguistic mediator, a god of ex-position and interpretation.[15] Julungul, by engaging in dialogue with all the snakes of the region, sets herself up as an arbiter, a clarifier. Her phallic origins in both *linga* and *herma* sets her up as an important purveyor of wisdom. This 'rising up' in the waterhole also implies a withdrawal from the lower and natural *yoni* represented by the shelter, and a reversal by means of which the phallus is pointed towards the Sun. Julungul has turned away from her hylic origins towards the supreme principle of intellect as it is embodied in language.

Swallowing the Women

Once again we find ourselves confronting the motif of regurgitation. As we have already seen in the Ankotarinja myth the dog-man was forced to give up or 'vomit' the *tilpa* men. So too does Julungul find herself in the position of giving back to the world the inert figures of the Wauwalak Sisters. Eliade regards the entry into the belly of a monster as equivalent to a regression into primal indistinctness, into the cosmic Night. To emerge from the monster signifies a cosmology. — to pass from an inchoate condition into that of an Absolute Form.[16] It is true that the neophytes, when they find themselves swallowed by the monster, go down into darkness where they are taught the secret traditions of the tribe. The fact that the Wauwalak Sisters are bitten into life by ants is a common motif for conveying the idea of rebirth as fully initiated beings. The formal separation of sons from their mother normally precedes the Kunapipi ceremonies, signifying a basic message of independence: 'This boy is your offspring. We must take him now and destroy his attachment to you. Then we will [re]-produce him as one of us.'[17] The young boys are reborn into the world as fully initiated men. Julungul becomes the instrument of rebirth when she vomits up the Wauwalak Sisters, breaks them into pieces with her song-stick, and swallows them over and over again. She exacts their total submission by resorting to her sceptre of words, her song-stick. It becomes clear that the sacred songs of the tribe are the true arbiter of all initiatative activity: a man must submit to the traditions of the tribe completely if he is to enjoy the prospect of rebirth.

By the act of consuming the sisters Julungul finds herself overcome with guilt feelings. Perhaps these women were her relatives, *dua* or *jiritja*, she thinks. Aware that in her unity she also embraces multiplicity, this becomes the intrinsic concern of the Great Snake. She must always ask this question and so provoke the tension of opposites which resides in her being. Rising again from the waterhole and spitting forth lightning and water, allowing thunder to roll from within her, her show of force reiterates the process of renewal. The Wauwalak Sisters

105

have been sacrificed in order that nature might be renewed. Rain and flood bring new life to a parched land. The Great Snake, by consuming a 'pair of opposites' in the form of Virgin and Mother, resolves this tension in a way that benefits the world.

She resorts to subterfuge. She tells all the snakes from afar that she has eaten everything but the sisters. Kangaroo, birds, even fish become a substitute for the truth — that she has consumed something *maraiin* or sacred. She has drawn into her being sacred knowledge. The Wauwalak Sisters represent that knowledge; they are the principle of esotericism, the secret knowledge pertaining to death-and-rebirth, to regeneration. Julungul, when she finally descends into the pool at Muruwul, and later withdraws into the distant cave from which she is never to re-emerge, is withdrawing into the power that is herself. Returning to her subterranean home, having been for so long the power that worked in the world outside it, she becomes forever hidden, and lost to the silence that gave birth to her in the first place. Her primordial unconsciousness, after it had clothed itself for awhile with words and with gestures, and ruled for a short period as the conscious, returns in silence to its own slumber in her uroboric being. Julungul withdraws from the world, aware that she is the repository of all things sacred. She is swallowed up by the abyss after participating in the cosmic drama of renewal. Her disappearance into the pool and the cave mysteriously echoes her own consumption of the Wauwalak Sisters. Thus layer upon layer of interpretation gathers about these protagonists, binding them more securely to one another.

In the end her final statement affirms her role in the creation of culture: "To you I give my ceremonies." The Kunapipi ceremonies are her gift to humankind. Not only do they embody her message to the world, but they encapsulate the forms of religious expression, so that all men can partake of her primeval essence. The rich earth of her personality is inculcated into the living by way of ritual and song. Her power as a rain-bringer overcomes the sterility of the land, and so brings about an abundance of food. The weather as an embodiment of principial virtue is drawn into this homologue. Snake, sisters and climate become a glorious triumvirate depicting the withdrawal of spirit from matter (drought) and its subsequent return (flood) after the enactment of the rituals (dance). Avataric and sublime, Julungul presides over a divine marriage between herself in her masculine incarnation as the phallus, and her bride, the Wauwalak Sisters huddled in their shelter. Because of its ability to cast off its skin, the snake is a symbol of renewal, a sun-symbol, which in turn can only beget itself. Julungul, though she is female throughout the myth, is in reality masculine. This act of concealment behind the veil of femininity is typical of mythopoiesis: the Great Snake adopts a disguise in order to protect his true identity from the gaze of the uninitiated. Rather than being a destroyer, a consumer of men, Julungul is a being who unites. According to the ancient Egyptians, the serpent's name 'Tum' is derived from the verb *num*, meaning 'to combine or unite.'[18] This is the true role of the Great Snake as he over-reaches the world.

The climax of the Kunapipi ceremonies for the young men comes in the form of their own sacrifice at the hands of Julungul. They are placed in a long trench which is said to represent the womb of Gungman, the elder Wauwalak Sister, the giver of birth. Then they are covered with bark and allowed to fall asleep. The men place two large cylindrical representations of Julungul on the edge of the trench. At a particular moment the bark is stripped off the boys so that they can witness the two objects towering above them. The Julungul effigies are then allowed to fall across the trench and the lads are lifted out.

The ceremony ends when the men emerge from the *nongaru* ground and reveal the new-born youths to the women. This action centres on two vertical forked posts connected by a horizontal pole decorated with branches. The women and children lie on the ground nearby, covered with mats, while two men perched in the forks cry out like new-born babes. The main body of men dance around the structure. At a given signal the women sit up and see the novices emerge from beneath the bushes (where they have been concealed). All of them are covered with red ochre symbolising blood from the Wauwalak Sister's uterus. That night the men dance around the youths and then lead them back to the sacred ground. Later, they all return to the general camp. From now on the initiates must live in the bachelor section.

The Kunapipi ceremony ends. We, on the other hand, find ourselves still immersed in the pool at Muruwul along with the Great Snake, Julungul, and his tribe of agathodaemon snakes. A sense of catharsis pervades the air. Though none of us has ever undergone ritual initiation, deep in our being we acknowledge the feeling of exhilaration that must inevitably accompany such a ceremony. Baptism, First Communion, even the ceremonies attached to the formal entry into a Lodge, in these there are distant echoes of the change of status that initiation embodies. We sense that in the Wauwalak myth the transition from childhood to manhood is inscribed. A great cosmic drama has been played out before our eyes. The Divine Phallus has impregnated our psyches with all the elements necessary to live a rich and full inner life. Rising rigidly towards the heavens, Julungul affirms the pure act of aspiration as central to life. We are conscious also of her initial unwillingness to reveal the meaning of life — at least until she has consumed its principal virtue herself. She is the Magician who lurks obscure and hidden away in the Waters. Until she is 'hewn apart' the Serpent withholds the flood, and will not propel the waters to the sea. This is the nature of her contradictory character. She reveals only what can be extracted from her by way of rite and ritual. These are the tools by which her *maraiin*, her sacredness, is acquired. The voice within, the voice of the Wauwalak Sisters, and therefore of femininity, speaks to humankind through the language of division and comparison. Julungul has given us the ability to recognize shades of meaning through the use of language. It is not inconceivable to see her as the inventor of language for the Aboriginal people, since she was at pains to identify each word spoken by the babble of snakes at her doorstep. *Dua* and *jiritja*, the principle of division and particularization, lie under her sphere of influence. Her bisexuality reinforces this also.

The Wauwalak Sisters affirm the importance of a number of ritual and mythic elements. In our rush towards psychic independence we have forgotten how to pay tribute to the invisible forces that govern nature itself. These forces are at work all the time in our lives, even though we have lost the ability to observe their *modus operandi*. In our eyes nature has become passive, a spirit broken by continual exploitation. We no longer subscribe to ceremonies which invoke nature as an active partner in the divine marriage. This is unfortunate because it has led to a situation where we see ourselves as existing independent of our environment. We no longer exist *in* nature, the world, but are content to create our own world in the mind. All our technological, scientific, social and political creations are projections of this world. They have become a substitute for what we are no longer able to extract from nature. Once the source of all our needs, and representing an equal partner in the business of living, nature has been reduced to the status of coolie by our obsessive need to recreate interior worlds. No more is it able to contribute on an equal footing to the full flowering of life.

Julungul and the Wauwalak Sisters remind us of how necessary it is to participate in a rite of passage at some time in our lives. We have yet to know what it is like to be consumed by a principial virtue which enables us to transcend our predicament. In contrast, every Aboriginal youth is required to confront such a condition when he lies in the trench at the foot of the snake effigies. He must lie there, buried under bark, his thoughts interiorised, fearing for his life, uncertain of his future. He must learn how to let the child in him die so that he may become a man. He must learn how to give up his dependence on his mother, and the threat her excessive caring and love poses to his spiritual growth. He must reject her overwhelming femininity which has been a part of his life until this point, and claim his birthright as a man, a warrior and hunter. Allowing himself to be consumed by the Great Snake, in whose belly he encounters sapiential knowledge for the first time, he is brought in contact with his essential maleness at last.

This is the lesson the Wauwalak Sisters can teach us, even today: that their disappearance into the alimentary tract of the serpent instils in us all a measure of sanctity, the knowledge of sacred things. We too bear within us things that are *maraiin*, which in turn may condition all our thought and action. Ultimately every word we utter is conditioned by the knowledge that the Spirit resides in us in the form of two sisters who refuse to allow themselves to be digested, and so go away. They must be constantly brought up, pummelled, and made digestible again. They who stand at the door to the Underworld, weaving their net of illusion, confront us with images of death and the need to transcend our material limitations. These women, the virgin and mother that intimate love, caring, birth and growth, are inviting us to join with them in a cosmic dance of renewal. Lightning and thunder orchestrate this dance, sending forth to the world fecundating rains, a cleansing downpour designed to precipitate new life on earth. This is their message. They bring forth the Waters of Life into a parched and needy world.

For the Aborigines of the north the Kunapipi rites remain a precious ornament. They embody the symbolism of Genesis and the Crucifixion combined. In a tribal context they make it possible to come together as one body. The *dua* and *jiritja* classification is shed, and people no longer see themselves as being separated by cultural restraints. They have become merged in the mythic event in a way that allows them to fulfil themselves as newly realized initiates. Boys are removed from their mothers, and then return to them as men. In the act of separation a more significant gift is bestowed. This loss of childhood signals the beginning of a new phase in life — that of participating in the task of renewing cultural and tribal affiliations for the benefit of the next generation. The great uroboric cycle of unity is maintained.

Swallowing the Women

Wherever we go in the world, we find that Muruwul waterhole, as deep as it appears, is always ready to yield up its knowledge in the form of Julungul, the Divine Phallus and progenitor of truth.

Part lll:
Among the Cloud Men

CHAPTER 9
Wandjina Country

Wandjina, you are telling me
Why do you lie to me?
Then cease your lying to me
Papa, please

Drrrrr....[1]

In the northwest of Australia lies a region known as the Kimberley. Much of the landscape there is of pre-Cambrian origins, although certain mountain chains such as the King Leopold Ranges indicate the existence of underwater reefs which today form dramatic landmarks in the wake of the sea's retreat, following periods of Ice-age inundation as recently as 20,000 years ago. The Kimberley is a mixture of hard, igneous rock, mysterious gorges which cut through ancient reef outcrops, remote rivers which become awash during the monsoon rains each year, and stony grasslands bearing a thin overlay of smaller eucalypts and shrubs. It is a hard, brooding landscape, a landscape filled with striking geological contrasts that for many express an inexplicable beauty. The Kimberley's grandeur lies partly in its remoteness, as well as the fact that it is the home of the Wandjina, a remarkable spirit-being which presides over the spiritual life of the local Aborigines.

The first white person to enter this region was the British explorer, George Grey. His party rode on horseback into the Kimberley in 1838, hoping to discover new pastoral country. During the early 1880s the Kimberley was gradually settled by intrepid overlanders who had brought their cattle many thousands of miles from eastern Australia, across unexplored and often dangerous country. Attacks by Aborigines were not infrequent. In time men like the Durack brothers established pastoral holdings which were to become a significant part of

Australian history and folklore. Often dismissive of the Aboriginal inhabitants, these pioneers built their ranches by sacred waterholes and grazed their herds on land which had belonged to the Kimberley tribes for many thousands of years. They were the new overlords who had come to supplant the sacred law of the Wandjina with the aid of stockwhip and gun.

Grey is reputed to be the first white man to set eyes on the Wandjina in their remote rock sanctuaries. Attempting to find a route down from a sandstone ridge into what appeared to him to be a 'fertile valley' one day, he happened upon some native fires which immediately alerted him to the presence of Aborigines. 'Looking over some branches, at the sandstone rocks which were above us,' he related in his journal, 'I suddenly saw from one of them a most extraordinary large figure peering down upon me. Upon examination, this proved to be a drawing at the entrance to a cave, which, on entering, I found to contain, besides, many remarkable paintings.' Grey had encountered the grave-looking visage of a Wandjina for the very first time.[2]

He later went on to record this encounter between himself and perhaps the most ancient image of deity that the world knows: 'I was certainly rather surprised at the moment that I first saw this gigantic head and upper part of a body bending over and staring grimly down at me.' Furthermore he said that it was 'impossible to convey in words an adequate idea of this uncouth and savage figure.' All he could do was measure its head and face, and record its 'length from bottom of face to navel.' In his description he did attempt a comparison however: 'Its head was encircled by bright red rays, something like the rays which one sees proceeding from the sun, when depicted on the sign-board of a public house; inside of this came a broad stripe of very brilliant red, which was coped by lines of white, but both inside and outside this red space, were narrow stripes of a still deeper red, intended probably to mark its boundaries; the face was painted vividly white, and the eyes black, being however surrounded by red and yellow lines; the body, hands and arms were outlined in red — the body being curious painted with red stripes and bars.'

It was not until the noted anthropologist, A.P. Elkin, had returned from his expedition into the region in 1927,[3] did the world begin to view these cult images as representing something more than Grey's 'savage and uncouth figures.' Elkin's studies, combined with those of later observers, began to unveil to the world the existence of a significant and very powerful cult image painted on cave walls throughout the Kimberley region. Elkin was able to ascertain that these caves were often storehouses for the bones of tribal elders considered to have been of cultural influence during their lifetime. An aura of death surrounded such places. The bones of these men, some of whom were said to have been living incarnations of the Wandjinas themselves, lay alongside great cloud-like spirit images, their ochred remains a constant reminder to others of the interplay between gods and men.

These Wandjina images do not appear to be located throughout the Kimberley region. They are roughly confined to the northwest, in an area bordered by the Drysdale River to the east, the King Leopold Ranges to the south, and the Indian Ocean to the west. Many of the Wandjina caves are located along the coast, leading to suggestions that the Wandjinas were a migrant cult which had arrived on Australian shores along with a secondary horde of Aborigines, said to have crossed over from Indonesia. Many beliefs in this region embody multiple characteristics that imply more than one set of cult-heroes existing alongside one another. Aside from the Wandjinas, images of Galaru, Walanganda (who is identified with the Milky Way) and other serpent heroes such as Ungud exist here.[4] Quite often this link is acknowledged by the Aborigines themselves, who often say that these Beings are really the same as one another. The Great Snake, Ungud, and the Wandjina often betray similar traits.

According to the Worora and Naringin peoples the Wandjina paintings are the imprints of the Sky Heroes on the cave walls. They maintain that during the time of the Dreaming (*Lalan*) the earth and all its natural features were created by these spirit-beings. Even today numerous *manduwul* or 'spirit paths' crisscross the country, denoting the Dream journeys of these Wandjinas at the time of the Dreaming. The Wandjinas performed acts of creation, engaged in battles with fellow Wandjinas (and devils), then 'lay down' in various caves. This 'lying down', though it implies death, in reality records the cessation of the Wandjinas' world-creating activities. They disappeared into the rock-face, leaving their images on the wall. The Wandjina paintings are therefore not rendered by men at all; but rather men are required to touch up a painting in order to maintain its iconic presence. Since the paintings are not made by men's hands (*acheiropoietos*), it is evident that they are the physical embodiment of the Wandjinas here on earth. As one informant remarked: 'This is our painting and this is our country. Wandjina put it here for us. If I finish [i.e. die] this becomes your business. If you born again [i.e. have a son] then this belongs to him.' This clearly affirms the custodial role that men take in preserving the Wandjinas from generation to generation.

Maintaining a Wandjina centre is a task that falls to certain ritual custodians only. In order to become a custodian a man's spirit must have originated in the vicinity of the cave concerned. Such a spirit will have entered his father as a dream, and then subsequently entered his mother's womb. A man's spirit is intimately linked to a piece of country, his *unguru* place, which in turn makes that man responsible for the conservation and 'wellbeing' of his particular totemic terrain. For these men, this involves knowing the rituals and songs pertaining to the Wandjina caves on their land, as well as being responsible for ceremonial re-painting when the occasion arises. Such an event is often associated with rain-making ceremonies, or those linked to the increase of natural species — wild dogs (dingoes), kangaroos, foodstuffs such as yams and berries, even fish. Retouching a painting brings on rain-power which in turn promotes natural increase throughout the region. Babies are often connected with the wet season, because a man may 'find' or dream a baby in the rain and lightning which is coming down all around him. The caves are storehouses of numinous power, often known as *kurunba* or *djang*, which enables the Aborigines to interact with the invisible realm of the Dreaming.

Wandjinas have no mouths. While they have expressive eyes, it appears that they do not speak. Their silence is attributed to the fact that they have 'nothing more to say' about Creation. This idea is reinforced by a brief myth which states:

> Dadmanmara said, 'I am going to speak.' But another Wandjina known as Ralamara hindered him and he became speechless. Ralamara actually put his hand on Dadmanmara's mouth and *blotted it out* (our italics).[5]

Capell argues that Aborigines rarely paint figuratively, and therefore do not see the need to portray Dreaming heroes with mouths. But he ignores the fact that images of deities that are 'silent' are recorded in our own literature. We speak of the *verbum perfectum* of the Paraclete, for example,[6] and we know that Aeneas encountered figures in the Underworld who were forever silent (*silentum concilium... umbraeque silentes*).[7] It would seem that when the Wandjinas entered the cave wall they gave up the need to converse. In effect they became the 'unspoken' presence of deity presiding over all.

Another commentator,[8] after questioning several Aborigines as to whether there was any reason known to them for the absence of a mouth, drew forth the response, "He has no mouth." His informants gravely looked at one another and remarked, "He has no teeth also." But beyond that they could provide no reason for such a depiction. The commentator concluded, like Capell, that Aborigines did not portray figures with mouths — in spite of the fact that in his article he showed a well-executed drawing of a crocodile which included a mouth. Nor did these observers consider that the original reason for the non-depiction of a mouth may well have been lost to these men over the centuries, in the same way as certain laws governing

119

Medieval religious iconography are no longer familiar to us.

Social organization among the Kimberley tribes is governed by a system of belief known as totemism. A full explanation of totemism is beyond the scope of this book,[9] but suffice is to say that each tribe is divided into two 'parties' or symbolic groups through which all social interaction takes place. A man or woman is loyal to his totemic identity throughout his life, and he or she will not eat any of the totems associated with his or her moiety. Totemic solidarity is also evident in arrangements at a large camp where members of one moiety are separated by some natural feature, such as a gully, from members of another. The dual organization is also manifested when disagreements arise; members of one totem may take sides against those of another, even if this implies that a man must fight with his sister's son. Among the Naringin people, the names of these moieties are *amalad* and *ornad* respectively. These in turn are divided between two animals and birds each: the hill kangaroo and night-bird are associated with the former, while the long-legged kangaroo and rain-bird are associated with the latter.[10] It follows that an Aborigine regards his totem as his *kian* or mate. He goes through life in league with nature by way of his totem. Not only is it a system of delineating social identity, but it also inspires a system of ritual responsibility whose primary concern is the maintenance and increase of natural phenomena. In other words, totemism is a form of ecological management of tribal territory.

Totems are intimately associated with Wandjina galleries. It is in these sacred centres that rituals are practised in order to assure the increase of such animals or species for the good of the tribe generally. While a man might not partake of his own totem, he is nonetheless responsible for its increase on behalf of his fellow tribesmen. In practice, however, a taboo can be broken by allocating the totems of his own tribal moieties to those of a horde situated comparatively far off from his country. The principle of 'out of sight, out of mind' occasionally comes into play, allowing for flexibility with regard to the eating or noneating of one's totemic mate, particularly in times of severe food shortage. Wandjina centres are associated with increase ceremonies, while at the same time being repositories of spiritual power laid down by the Wandjinas themselves. Their heroic endeavours at the time of the Dreaming, and their subsequent disappearance, make these power-centres important ritual and meditation sites. They can even be associated with curative medicine in the case of those who might be suffering from coughs and colds. It is said that a man passing certain power-places will not sneeze. Indeed if a man dreams (i.e. meditates) in such a location, he is able to shrug of any ailment that is affecting him.[11]

Relying on the power of dreams as a divinatory aid is important to the Kimberley tribespeople. If a family has been spending time with another group far from their kin, for example, one of the parents might experience their kin's concern in a dream. Before leaving their hosts, the tribesman might say, "We have been long with your people now, and you have looked after us. But my sinews are tired; they tell me to return to our people." When they had returned to their people, they might learn that their family had been experiencing a vision of their *dji* or totem also. "I dreamt of a snake last night, so maybe our son is coming."[12] In fact, they might have even brought in extra food, knowing that their return was imminent.

The Wandjina's link with rain and severe weather upheaval is well attested. The word itself is derived from the widely found root *wan, wun, win,* meaning 'water'. Wandjina literally means 'near the water' (cf. Ungud, which derives from the same root, means 'from the water').[13] In the Garirinja cave the mere touching of the painting is said to cause hurricanes. The mysterious headgear Wandjina wears was initially regarded as containing 'indecipherable script' by European observers, perhaps recounting the distress calls of shipwrecked sailors marooned along the coast during the nineteenth century. But Aborigines are adamant that what look like written characters are the symbolic marks of lightning. As one informant remarked with reference to painting and retouching Wandjina pictures, "Lightning came first, before the Wandjina. Black cockatoo feathers that emerge from his crown represent it too."[14] Which leads us to conclude that the Wandjina are intimately associated with rain and the beginning of the monsoon season. Furthermore, the vertical stripes often seen on the bodies of Wandjinas represent falling rain.

We are therefore in the presence of a significant Sky Hero whose primary reason for existence is to augment the rainy season. But to see the Wandjinas solely as increase cult-heroes is to discount their metaphysical importance entirely. It is clear that the Wandjina centres act as pilgrimage points to which initiated men travel prior to the wet season in order to enact sacred rituals and to retouch the paintings. By classifying these places in terms of their spiritual significance, they are able to give a physical dimension to their totemic country which serves as a link to their ancestors. It must be remembered that for Aborigines landscape embodies little until it suggests a Dreaming identity. By visiting a place associated with a metaphysical event a tribesman is able to imbue his life with certain verities which he is able to travel towards, both in the act of walking and in his thoughts. The causal relationship between repainting and bringing on the rainy season is of ritual significance only, since it allows Aborigines to participate in the process of nature as a helpmate. Such acts of sympathetic magic are designed to affirm the interdependence of humankind and nature to the extent that each requires the other if cosmic harmony is to be maintained.

Which leads us to the question of Wandjina mythogenesis. Here indeed we find ourselves entering a new field of investigation. The Wandjina myths of the Kimberley are unlike other mythic narratives in Australia. In many ways they strike us as being perhaps the rawest of all myths, as if they hide no message but their inordinate penchant for describing journeys and naming places. Some of them, however, do seem to reflect the principles of cultural and social behaviour when such issues were in their formative stage. This in itself makes these myths fascinating, because we find ourselves in the presence of that pristine moment when people first tried to account for their own behaviour. It is as if we sense that glorious occasion when events, thoughts, and motives became objectified for the very first time. A kind of innocence pervades those actions surrounding the doings of the Wandjinas. We begin to tremble in anticipation as they describe the way the world is named at the time of the Dreaming. In the following excerpts from two myths we begin to encounter the primordial moment of Creation, and the process of identifying places for all time:

> At Ilili, we'll sit down and stretch open our vagina with our fingers. So the women sat down on a flat rock in the shade by the water. Then they stretched opened their vaginas with their fingers. They all opened their legs and stretched them wide. They called the place Ilililinjari, because they opened them there. "Yes," they said. "We opened them there." And they called that place the Stretching Place.[15]

Here we have an account of how a particular place received its Dreaming identity. The piece of country known as Ililinjari, the Stretching Place, is associated with the activities of female Wandjinas who touched their genitalia in a gesture which accounted for the naming of the place. In spite of its clear sexual overtones, we begin to sense the presence of an untrammeled freedom at work in this explanation, as if the actions of the Wandjinas constituted an inquiry into their own gender rather than any inclination towards masturbatory pleasure. The wonder of body is ever present. The women have no qualms about glorying in their gender as they touch themselves. The place becomes a memorial to that first encounter we have with self-awareness, with seeing ourselves as unique and different. The Stretching Place becomes a perpetual reminder of this event for Aborigines: They are able to re-create that Dreaming event when their women perceived themselves as 'different'. The concept of duality in the form of sexual difference was enshrined at Ilililinjari.

123

In the second excerpt we have:

> Starting off next day, Waningiyalu passed through this place and proceeded eastward. He climbed along Ngurini Range. Then he followed the river, walking on the plain.
>
> "Never mind, I'll camp for awhile," he said as the sun began to set.
>
> When night fell, Waningiyalu arose and looked about with some surprise.
>
> "Oh, it's dark! What's this spreading darkness all about me? It's pitch black," he said. "I'll call this camp Manayirung (i.e. pitch dark)." So that's what he named the place.
>
> Next day he followed along the top side of the river. Passing the place where the frog croaked, he called it Djarunmalan. He continued to travel on the flat. He followed the creek to Bindilu where the Wandjina, Bilimar, first appeared. Where the Wandjina laid down was named after him.[16]

Again we are presented with that moment of pristine recognition when the concept of darkness was realized. Another place bears the name of the frog's croak in honour of this event. When we reach Bindilu we have arrived at a sacred place where a Wandjina has disappeared into the cave wall. Darkness, a sound from nature, and the completion of a Dream journey by a world-creator reverberate throughout this brief narrative. It is as if we are stepping forth into that archaic landscape where nothing yet has occurred *outside time*. The entire world is new. No overlay of culture is present. Darkness, a frog's croak and a journey constitute primordial events from which the original inhabitants of the continent were able to build up a picture in which they could identify themselves. Moreover it is important to recognize that at some point *in* time men found it necessary to put together the mosaic of celestial events that occurred time, so that they too might begin to measure their own emergence as distinct beings on this earth. At Bindilu we have the sense that real events took place at the time of the Dreaming which even now affect us at a deeper level of our consciousness.

We must remember, however, that the Wandjina is a

multifaceted being. He is both a spirit in the normal sense, a man (or woman) in another sense, and an animal or natural species in a third sense. His progress across the land of the Kimberley is conditioned by what he embodies at a physical level, and what he alludes to at the metaphysical level. He is also a cosmological being in that he presides over the monsoon rains, as well as creating topographic landmarks. The Aborigines depict him as a cloud-like being, but they also acknowledge his invisibility as a spirit. At the iconic level they account for his presence in the world in a number of forms. The Wandjina is said to be a) the frontal suture in a baby's head b) the neckbone in a freshwater turtle c) a small transparent lizard, and finally d) frog spawn is regarded as reflecting the eye of the Wandjina. It means that the Wandjina is ever-present in the daily lives of Kimberley tribespeople in the natural artifacts that surround them. They do not have to visit the sanctuaries to encounter the spirit of the Wandjina. He exists near them and, to a certain extent, within them. He is *ungud* — a spiritual condition which links him to divinity itself. Things and events that partake of *ungud* are what we might classify as sacred.

To discover the mystery of these spirit beings, we must be prepared to enter their territory and encounter them on their own terms. We must be prepared to wander the sacred landscape of the Kimberley and stub our toes on their creation-myths. Standing under a rock overhang at Wanalirri in order to witness the hieratic gaze of Wodjin will certainly bring us closer to his particular ground of being, his *raison d'etre*.[17] Mythogenesis involves an act of courage too. It requires us to embark upon an interior journey along the disused paths of our own primordial consciousness. We have to be able to understand what it is like to observe the dark for the first time, to discover fire, to bury our dead, indeed to enjoy all aspects of reality as symptoms of that state of pristine recognition already alluded to. As one informant remarked: 'Wandjina is the important one. He made the world.'

It is important to begin this journey. The Kimberley region offers us the chance to tramp along gullies filled with the petrified bones of our mythic forebears. Let us first stand at the foot of Ngalenga hill, a remote outcrop on the Roe River, where the Wandjina named Nangina, or the 'Man of Darkness' (*nang-ina* the night or darkness man. *Nang-un* = night. *Nangi* = darkness) is said to have emerged from the ground. Let us try to experience the world as he saw it, gazing as he did with wide, charcoal-black eyes. His white face, resplendent in its aureole of red ochre rays, gives no hint of his surprise. Nangina gazes at us from the rock face, and we are immediately entranced. For he has chosen us to become his custodians as we enter into the spirit of his mythogenic world-birth.

CHAPTER 10
Ngalenga Hill

The myth begins:

A CAVE APPEARS

Nangina emerged from the spinifex grass long before our time. He was sent by the Wandjina into our world from underneath the ground. When he came out, he named the hill Ngalenga.

He heard a noise and asked: "What is that rumbling?"

He continued to listen. Suddenly he saw something that he had never witnessed before. Standing before him was a devil who was chipping away at the rock-face in an attempt to gouge out a cave. Nangina decided to sneak up on the devil while the spirit was busy working on the soft rock.

"I must find out what is making this rumbling sound," he said.

Meanwhile the devil continued to dig out the cave. When he had finished, he lay outstretched on the ground inside the cave, his red penis hanging free. In that moment he became a painting.

"Oh yes, he's a devil, all right," Nangina said as he crept into the cave to observe the painting on the wall.

Nangina stood up to his full height. He marvelled at the painting. Then he composed a song:

> Let it be dark-moving!
> Let it be dark-looking!
> Let it be wide!
> Move! Move!

"The cave needs to be made wider," Nangina said.

As he spoke the cave suddenly grew bigger. The noise made as it expanded nearly deafened him. When the noise died down, Nangina could see that the cave was larger than before. He examined every nook and cranny, pronouncing it a suitable place to paint his signature. So he placed his outstretched hand on the rock-face and, filling his mouth with white ochre, spray-painted his hand on the surface. Exhausted by his encounter with the devil, Nangina lay down in the cave and slept for three days.

Ngalenga Hill

YAMS

"First I'll try and dig up ome of these yams," Nangina said.

With a loud, crunching noise he soon began to eat them. In time his mouth became sticky.

"What have I eaten?" he cried. "Ouch! Still, I must take them back to camp."

Nangina carried the yams in a bark dish. He decided to rest for a short time while he thought about the yams. Meanwhile the sun caused the juice in the yams to grow hot. Nangina tasted the juice. Then he rubbed his sticky hands on a flat stone.

"Now my hands are hot too!"

He stacked the juicy yams in a pile before he lay down to rest.

MAKING FIRE

"I'll try and cut down that tree," Nangina said. Then he broke the sapling apart in order to study its texture. He smelled the scent of eucalypt.

"This is the one, all right. This is the one," he said, scraping the bark from the stick.

Then Nangina chipped a piece of stone and bored a small hole in it. He spun the stick around in this hole to make it smooth.

"Now I want to cut a groove on another piece of stick so that the pith dust can fall through," he said, proudly observing his handiwork.

Presently he poured a few grains of sand into the groove, placed the stick in the groove also, and then twirled it around rapidly with his hands like a drill. The pith wood became hot with the movement of the stick against the sand in the groove. Smoke rose from the groove.

"Here it comes!" Nangina said as he continued to twirl the wood.

A small glow appeared in the groove.

"Hey, what will I do with it now?" he asked. Casting about, he found some kindling, and sprinkled pieces of decayed wood on the flame. Nangina began to blow until a small flame shot up. Then he poured the burning coals onto the kindling. Within minutes he had stoked the tiny flame into a fire.

"How about that?" he said, a note of pride in his voice.

COOKING YAMS

With a digging stick Nangina cleaned out an earth oven into which he placed the juicy yams. Then he covered the pile with ashes and hot coals, commencing on the left side before covering the right side. While the yams were baking, Nangina lay down and slept. When he awoke, he felt a little lightheaded. He was excited by the prospect of his first meal of yams.

Opening the oven, he dragged out the yams and piled them in a heap. He smelt cooking aromas coming from the oven.

"This looks like good food," he said.

Finally he took a yam in his hand and squeezed it.

"Oh, it's soft," he said.

Laying the yams out to cool, Nangina arranged a flat stone on the ground. Presently he began to grind the yams into a fine powder on the stone.

"Now I'll try and eat it," he said.

As soon as he put the flour to his mouth, the flavour rose up through his nostril and ears. He could not believe how tasty it was.

"This is good," he said to himself.

Nangina had eaten enough. His stomach had swollen considerably. So he walked down to the creek to quench his thirst. His stomach grew even bigger. Hoping to relieve the feeling of indigestion, Nangina walked all the way home to Ngalenga hill, his home country, where he lay down again to sleep off his first meal of yams.

"Since I swelled up with this food," he announced. "I'll call it a 'yam'."

The word 'yam' was given to Aborigines by Nangina.

He created the word.

"Since Ngalenga is my home, it's where I made the word for yam. I will be famous," he added after a pause.

Nangina walked around the back of Ngalenga hill and named this place also.

"This is Wunbala, which means 'the rear of the hill.' It's mine. Because of me it's also famous," he said. Nangina noticed the aroma of yams. "I smell yam here. The smell is very strong." Leaning over, he smelt the scent of yam flowers.

"I name this place Wowaran, which means 'overpowering'." he said.

He walked about digging up more yams in the vicinity. One of these yams he broke open to reveal a strong white colour.

"How did it become white?" he asked. "Anyway, this place is mine, so I name it Danbamiri, which means 'the white place.' It will be famous like me."

Nangina then returned to camp.

Ngalenga Hill

DREAMING AND THE YAM PAINTING

In his dream Nangina was walking. Suddenly he saw a yam, the one he had cracked open with a stick, limping along. Finally he caught up with the yam, when it lay down in the Dreaming cave.

"I'm a bushy splitter," the yam said to Nangina.

"Ah hah, so you are," replied Nangina.

Nangina awoke while the dream was still fresh in his thoughts, and he said: "I want to find that cave where I saw the yam in my dream."

So Nangina headed off on a journey. Eventually he found the yam's cave. When he entered the place, he found the spirit of the yam imprinted on the rock-face.

He proceeded to draw more yams beside one another, their heads pointing downwards. He used red ochre, charcoal and pipeclay.

"I'll call this place Yalanba after the yam I saw limping along," he said. Because the rock was still soft he knew that holes had opened up to receive the sacred yams he had painted.

He left Yalanba where he had made these paintings.

FINDING A WIFE

Nangina was taking a walk one day. Presently he heard a strange noise coming from the river.

"Hey, what's that?" he asked. "It can't be birds. They don't cry like that. What is this noise? What are they crying about?"

In his dream Nangina peered over a ridge. Below he saw a group of women bathing in the water. He noticed one woman's breast glittering in the sunlight.

"My goodness," Nangina said. "That woman is beautiful. She looks all new. I better get hold of her."

He hurried down the slope and grabbed hold of the woman's arm as she came ashore. Then he dragged her away from the other women and made his escape.

Meanwhile the women fled the scene; but not before one of them had remarked: "Our friend has been taken by a devil, all right. That's the end of her."

That afternoon Nangina and his new wife camped together, after having stopped briefly at a creek to quench their thirst.

"You're my boss woman," he said to her. "I name you Njalbagud, which means 'broken arm', after what I did to you when I grabbed you from the water. I want to take you home to my place at Ngalenga."

Ngalenga Hill

Meanwhile the young Njalbagud decided to leave camp and dig for yams. Nangina took the opportunity to go out hunting kangaroo. When his wife returned with an armful of yams, she made a camp oven and cooked them. Nangina arrived a short time later and tossed down the carcase of a kangaroo at her feet.

"Oh," she said with admiration. "You've speared a kangaroo. Oh, my husband, my husband!" To show his appreciation Nangina offered Njalbagud a prime piece of fat which she cooked on the fire. He dug a pit for the kangaroo, singed the hair off its skin, cut off its tail, before pushing hot coals into the oven. While the kangaroo was cooking Njalbagud offered Nangina a piece of fat to eat. Later, when the kangaroo had cooked, they both sucked up the juices from its body. They covered the yams with coals again, and went to sleep.

FINDING A CHILD AND ITS BIRTH

In his dream Nangina rose and walked down to a waterhole. He heard a splashing sound made by spirit-babies as they played together in the water. Nangina drew closer, and for awhile watched them playing. Then one of the spirit-babies began to swim towards him. He crouched low in the swamp grass in an attempt to hide. The spirit-child stood up and casually leaned against the bank. Nangina reached out and grabbed the spirit-child from behind.

"Who are you?" he demanded.

"I'm Wulawodei," the spirit-child said.

Nangina tied Wulawodei on his head, and made his way back to camp. Then he lay down beside his wife, who was still sleeping. Carefully he untied the spirit-child from his head, and placed him on the top of Njalbagud's pubic hair. The spirit-child immediately entered the woman's body.

Days later Njalbagud awoke from a nap to find her stomach swollen.

"What's wrong with me?" she asked. "I don't feel too good."

"Don't you remember the little one I gave to you?" Nangina replied. "Didn't you see it?"

"Ah, so that's what has made me feel different," his wife said. "In a dream I saw the spirit-child drinking from my breasts."

"There you are!" Nangina said.

Njalbagud vomited a number of times after that. But she also noticed that her belly was growing bigger. It grew and grew. She even felt the child moving inside her. To give herself more strength in preparation for the coming birth, Njalbagud painted herself with

131

pipeclay.

"That will make it easier for me," she thought.

Meanwhile the child turned round inside her. The next day it was born. The child cried. Nangina helped his wife rub charcoal dust over the baby's body. Later, Njalbagud severed the umbilical cord and hung it around her neck.

The young boy soon grew. He struggled to his feet, toddled a few steps, then fell over again. Nangina offered Wulawodei a digging stick to lean on when he stood up. But most of the time Njalbagud carried him in her arms when they moved about.

When he grew bigger, his mother used to carry Wulawodei straddled over one shoulder, not around her neck. Pretty soon he was running about without her help. As he grew up, Wulawodei learnt how to play games. His mother cut him a small club to play with.

One day Nangina noticed a bush fire on the horizon. It was a hunting fire, presumably lit by someone else.

"You better stay here," Nangina said to his wife and son as he set out to investigate.

Presently Nangina discovered a band of tribesmen who had been hunting in the wake of the fire.

"Hey, here's Nangina. He's arrived at last," one of them announced.

Nangina politely sat down on the ground some distance from their camp, and waited for his family to catch up. Following his tracks, Njalbagud and Wulawodei arrived. They put their belongings on the ground and made a fire for him.

NANGINA FIGHTS

When darkness was upon them, the local tribesmen whispered among themselves: "Let's ask Nangina to sing his songs to us."

Nangina obliged by beating time with clap-sticks as he sang:

Move, move, let it be wide
Let there be darkness
Let there be an invisible rope!

The tribesmen gathered round to listen. The fire glowed. They pretended to enjoy what they heard. One man said:

"Oh! Your singing takes hold of my liver." Which really meant, 'You stir my feelings.' But Nangina did not know that the man was speaking hypocritically.

Ngalenga Hill

As he sang the tribesmen inched towards him. Such was his concentration that he did not notice them beginning to crowd in on him. Suddenly they all rushed at him, grabbing him around the throat. Some others held Nangina's arms and legs pinioned to the ground. Others rolled over his stomach, knocking the wind out of him. He became slippery with sweat as he struggled to overcome his foes. As soon as his sweat rubbed off on them he was able to slip from their clutches.

Nangina raised one man above his head and bashed his head against a slab of stone. The man lay there, his brains protruding from his fractured skull, his tongue hanging loose from his mouth. Next he raised another man and bashed him down on the stone also. He dealt with a third man in the same way, so that there were brains all over the place.

"Njalbagud, where are you!" Nangina cried out.

"Quick, bring me a spear and womera!"

Njalbagud rushed over to her husband with the weapons and gave them to him. Nangina hastily attached one spear to his womera and hurled it at another man. The man immediately fell to the ground, the spear lodged in his chest. He hooked up another spear and brought down a fifth man in the same way. He kept spearing men until there was no one left. Some had already fled. All around him lay dead bodies. Nangina sank to the ground, exhausted.

"Njalbagud, bring me fire," he called. Then he demanded: "Where is my son?"

Njalbagud gave her husband a fire-stick. Nangina and his son set out in a wide arc lighting fires. The burning grass crackled, sending up thick plumes of smoke. He did not burn in the direction of his cave at Ngalenga. Instead he burnt the grass in the opposite direction. Throughout the night he fired the grass until the entire region was aglow with flames.

By dawn he was finished. Nangina and his family made their way home to Ngalenga after that. Njalbagud crept inside first and moved away the yams that she had stored there, in order to make a clearing where they could lie down and rest. When Nangina arrived the heaps of yams were like sloping hills in the cave. They ate a big meal together.

Meanwhile those men who were not killed during the fight came looking for Nangina. The only place that had not been burnt by the conflagration was the cave at Ngalenga, so they made their way towards it. At the entrance to the cave they could smell the fire within. But they could not find Nangina and his family. They had taken refuge at the back of the cave.

"I wonder where he is?" one man said.

Presently they returned to the battlefield and gathered up the bodies of their dead. They made bark coffins for them and placed them inside. When they had completed this task, they carried their dead all the way back to the Wandjina painting where they heaped them at the entrance to the cave. Then they camped that night near the Wandjina painting.

In the morning they prepared for war again. Many men had gathered. Meanwhile they carried more of the bark bundles containing the corpses over to Muralan cave, where another Wandjina was painted. They stored them inside. Even today, the bones of these ancestors can still be seen near the Wandjina painting.

In the meantime Nangina, now a warrior, continued to live in his country with his family. Wulawodei soon grew to become a man. The two often went hunting together, spearing kangaroo to take home to eat. They all ate lots of yams sweetened with honey. As the years rolled on Nangina found his hair growing grey and his feet becoming unsteady when he walked. It was a long time now since he had fought those men and killed them with his bare hands. The memory troubled him.

"I better have words with them," he said to himself, thinking of the tribesmen who had survived.

At the same time, the tribesmen had sent word to Nangina to join them for a corroboree. When they saw the old man coming towards them through the scrub with the aid of a walking stick, they began to feel sorry for him. He was no longer the strong man they knew of earlier days. The Man of Darkness, the hermit of Ngalenga, looked like a grandfather to them.

So they talked to him and made their peace. No one attempted to hit him with a club or spear him. They just listened to him telling them his stories. In the end they followed him back to his secret cave at Ngalenga. When they arrived there, one of them called out:

"Nangina!"

He answered: "Aj!"

"We see smoke coming out of the cave. We don't recognize this place," another asked.

"What place?" Nangina pretended.

"Isn't that your place?" someone else called.

Then the tribesmen went forward and grabbed Nangina. He was struck on the neck with a club and he fell down, his neck broken. He lay there, 'altogether finished', a broken old man. The tribesmen left Ngalenga then, not wishing to molest either Njalbagud of Wulawodei.[1]

So ends the myth of Nangina. The man died in order to prevent a revenge killing of his son. He knew this might happen when he made the journey to the camp of his attackers. They in turn were aware of the need for some final sacrifice on his part so that their feud might be put to rest. This primal myth explores events and issue which are still with us today. Nangina, the first man, takes us on a journey which expresses all our primordial concerns, our pleasures, and our anguish. He experiences things *for the first time*. This is his great gift to us. As raw as his narrative seems it nonetheless conceals within it all the vital requirements of existence. Life, death, basic survival, the establishment of the social entity, acknowledgement of human affection, the making of a home, the emergence of negative human values in the form of hypocrisy and violence, followed by a desire for atonement — all these archetypes are framed within the myth. Nangina's journey of discovery echoes that of Odysseus, Arjuna, and many other mythic heroes of later times. Njalbagud could be the maiden Nausicaa whom Odysseus discovers by the stream when he steps ashore in Phaeacia. Nangina's battle with the tribesmen could be that of Odysseus doing battle with the suitors, or Arjuna with the Kauravas on the field of Truth. What we are witnessing is the first flowering of the mythogenic process. Nangina is our guide. He has allowed us to step inside his cave, graced as it is with the luminous paintings of Wandjina figures. We are staring at them, at their cloud-like faces, knowing that we too are in the presence of something special.

Simon of Taibutheh, a sixth-century Syrian saint, once remarked: 'Understanding and discernment are the instruments of knowledge.' By this he meant that we must not be too ready to accept the veracity of our immediate impressions. Somewhere beneath the surface of all mythic structure, like a crocodile lurking at the bottom of its pool, there lies a deeper knowledge,

Ngalenga Hill

a knowledge that cannot be fully realized except through understanding and discernment. Nangina, hunter and warrior that he is, is now ready to accompany us around the base of Ngalenga hill in order to reveal for the first time Wunbala — that is, the 'rear side of' this mythic mountain which is his home.

CHAPTER 11
The Man of Darkness

In the myth of Nangina we find ourselves witnessing the first moment of Creation much as we did when we observed the emergence of the Dog-man, Ankotarinja, from the dry riverbed at Ankota. Nangina is both Everyman and a god as he rises up out of the long spinifex grass at Ngalenga. He comes from deep within the earth, divinely directed by the Wandjina to engage fully in life. As the 'Man of Darkness' he expresses the primeval consciousness of someone who has not yet discerned the difference between night and day. He is an undifferentiated being, and one who is prepared to parade his innocence, oblivious to the envy of those that might wish him ill. His myth explores the tragedy of a man, indeed a god, who appears in the world bearing a divine message, and is cut down for his pains. He is the archetype of all Greek and Elizabethan theatrical tragedians, even Christ. He represents the very stuff from which all human suffering is fashioned. In every one of us a scintilla of Nangina's joy and despair resides. He has witnessed the wonder of world-creation, and yet lived long enough to see his own creation reduced to ashes. He has lived, loved, and died at the hands of his brothers so that a primal act of evil might be expunged from the face of the earth. This is the essence of his story — and the story of all men as they struggle to come to terms with the paradox of living in a world which on one level appears to be so perfect, while on another chooses to express itself by way of so much pain and suffering. The Primordial Power is forever at play, creating, preserving, and destroying. Nangina finally discovers this to be true at the cost of his own life.

It is important to understand where Nangina is coming from. Even as he names things and presides over the rumbling noise of Creation, he is aware that a devil has entered the world. That this devil is intent upon digging his own grave wherein he transforms himself into a painting must not detract from what he is really doing. After all, he is content to dig out a cave which Nangina immediately recognizes as being too small for human, or indeed divine habitation. The world must be made much larger if cosmic events are to be enacted to the full. In the presence of the painting he therefore calls upon the Wandjina to make the cave larger in accordance with his vision of the world. 'Let it be dark-moving! Let it be wide! Move! Move!' becomes a magical incantation uttered, so to speak, at the entrance to Aladdin's cave. And so the cave grows larger — large enough to receive Nangina's vote of approval. His 'signature' not only indicates the possession of the cave in his name, but also that he has taken possession of the world in the name of all humankind. His ochred hand imprint on the wall signals that he is no longer content to be a mere observer of cosmic events any more. From now on he wishes to become a participant in the business of world-creation.

The devil's penis on the cave wall alerts us to the presence of the divine Phallus. So that this devil is not a 'devil' as such, but in truth is a Wandjina. The cave becomes a shrine to the potency of nature. Nangina acknowledges this when he marvels at the painting. He is in the presence of deity, the cloud-faced figure of a Wandjina. His song is addressed to the Wandjina, imploring the spirit-being to make the world 'wider', more complete, so that he might explore its wonders at his leisure. The Man of Darkness fills his mouth with liquid pipeclay, said to promote strength among Aborigines, and sprays this mystical substance over the symbol of his eternal presence (his hand) placed beside the image of the Wandjina. The two are now one. Wandjina and Dreaming hero are ready to encounter the world as it is. After three days of slumber, his journey of discovery is ready to begin.

How pristine is that moment when Nangina digs up his first yams. Here before him lies his first encounter with the nutritious aspect of the earth. As he tries to eat them raw they make a noise, and his mouth becomes sticky. He is at a loss as to how to deal with his first taste of food. The sun makes the juice in them too hot to taste. We are made aware of his confusion when his hands are burnt by the yam juice. This is very likely what happened when the first hunter-gatherer dug up these roots, and considered what he was to do with them. The first man, in this case Nangina, needed to work out a new plan of attack. As yet the yams had not yielded up their nutriment, though they had intimated such a possibility. In this sense these roots embody the highest principle of all, which manifests itself in food. According to Hindu belief, Brahman, the divine essence makes itself known to the priestly seer (i.e. Nangina) in the following way:

> I am the first born of the divine essence.
> Before the gods sprang into existence, I was.
> I am the navel of immortality.
> Whoever bestows me on others — thereby keeps me to himself.
> I and FOOD. I feed on food and on its feeder.[1]

Nangina encountered his food in its raw state and found it wanting. The next stage of his journey involved the discovery of fire, the very essence of all transformative processes.

The interlude where Nangina discovers how to make fire is perhaps one of the most moving events related in the myth. Reading this passage, we find ourselves as if gazing through the wrong end of a telescope. The event seems so distant from us, and yet we know that it must have occurred at some unique point in time. A man discovered for himself how to rub two sticks together and make fire. He learnt by practical demonstration one of the laws of modern thermology: that friction causes heat and thereby energy. By rubbing two sticks together, and introducing a friction agent in the form of sand, Nangina discovered how to create and to control energy. He was able to draw forth the fire lying dormant in the wood itself. He had made a principial discovery: that in his hands lay the possibility of transforming one substance into another. The management of fire represents the beginning of a new life for him. He is now ready to embark on a career as a fire-maker, a heat inducer, a transformer of the raw into the cooked.

This event alone signals a significant step. Nangina had realized a lack in his life. Clearly he was not satisfied with the taste of uncooked yams. He was looking for something more. He wanted to improve the quality of his life. Fire became the catalyst for him. In so doing he was able to align himself with the energy of Creation — that is, heat. We see Nangina as Agni, the god of the sacrificial fire, the embodiment of Surya, the sun, as portrayed in Vedic mythology. 'The fire, breathing forth and upward, enters into the wind.' So too does Nangina, the fiery messenger of the gods, teach us how fire is made. Its discovery is reported in the *Aitareya Brahmana* (Rg Veda) in a similar vein:

> Thence are these deities born again; from the wind is born the fire [fire churned by means of a stick twirled in a hole nicked in a board; the stick is of hard wood, the board of softer; the little flame alights on the board — as it were out of air]; for from breath (*prana*) it is born, being kindled by strength. [The wind is the form of the life-breath-energy (*spiritus, prana*) within man, joined to bodily strength (*bala*) though man's exertion during the process of churning actually produces fire.][2]

Furthermore, we are made aware of how Nangina came to notice the transformative nature of fire. His encounter with the hot juice of the yams drew his attention to this process. The divine spark of an idea was imbedded in nature itself. In turn this was activated by the heat from the sun. His great discovery was to realize that fire was associated with wood, with the heat of the living cell. He made fire by twirling a stick of hardwood in a hole notched into a softer plank. The rotation produced heat and presently a park. This was comparable to the process of generation: the twirling spindle of the plank were the fire's parents, respectively male and female; therefore fire was the 'offspring' of wood. The wood grew and was the 'grandchild of water', making it the water's child, since it had been born of lightning from the watery womb of the clouds. In all living things fire abides and is recorded by the temperature of the body.

Nangina discovered this when he 'burnt' his fingers while touching the yam juice. As a result he was able to identify the manifestation in the microcosm of the macrocosmic fire. Nangina had taken upon himself the responsibility of a man of knowledge, a priest, such is the power of his new knowledge. Is it any wonder that he exclaims: "How about that?" as the full significance of his discovery dawns upon him?

Now is the time for Nangina to apply this newly acquired knowledge, this 'wisdom of the fire'. We note that he prepares his camp oven in which he lays his yams with due care. The coals and sand are heaped first from the left, then from the right. The rite of cooking has become second nature to him. Already he has attained to a state of being where 'everywhere and every when is focused' (Dante). He is following a pattern of action in order to change the condition of his yams. There is a sense of anticipation in which the future becomes a virtually already existent reality, so that the future transformation of the raw to the cooked stage is actually present. All this implies a conception of time and space that is not in our sense of the word 'rational': instead one in which both past and future, cause and effect, coincide in a present experience. It is evident that Nangina's ritual actions give him a certain control over the outcome of his endeavours. No wonder he felt lightheaded when he awoke; he had, for the first time, formalized an action in order to realize a desired purpose.

We see him opening the oven and piling the cooked yams on the ground. It is a moment when he contemplates the success of his actions. The pleasant aroma of cooked food tantalises him, and makes him believe that all his work has been worthwhile. He is inspired to try something new — that is, to manufacture flour from the yams. Already we see him establishing the rudiments of culture, giving form to the practical details of living. Here is a man *transforming* himself in his act of changing the criteria by which he lives. It is a significant moment in the life of a god come down to earth: he is making sacrosanct knowledge, the wherewithal of survival. Nangina, the first man, a Wandjina of

141

eternal presence, tastes the simple yam cake for the first time. Its flavour captivates him. All his senses are stimulated. In that instant the opacity of the world has been made more diaphanous by the introduction of an entirely new sensation. How can he not fail to over-indulge his new passion by eating too much? Desire and satiation are inextricably linked. He consumes more than he needs. Thirstily he casts about for water in an attempt to alleviate his discomfort. Only then does he encounter the expansive nature of flour when it is subject to the digestive process. As a result he learns an important lesson: that indulgence leads to a constriction of his being from which he can only escape by 'sleeping it off'. In other words, too much of anything leads to a state whereby the realm of unconsciousness begins to encroach once more, negating all that hard-won knowledge so far attained.

Home is where he must return in order to regain his equilibrium. He contemplates his error, and resolves to identify it for all time by naming the 'yam'. Thus he is able to preserve the inherent qualities of the yam, both positive and negative. He perpetuates the intrinsic nature of the yam in its name. The yam is recognized and empowered. Nangina, the seer and high priest, is now ready to extend his domain. He begins to name other places, and things. In naming Wunbala as the 'rear of the hill', he acknowledges the importance of dimension in life, the 'other side' or 'hidden depth' of knowledge. He acknowledges also his egoity, the birth of his self-consciousness in this act. From now on he will be 'famous', a man of distinction, someone that the rest of humankind will remember with reverence.

This state of exemplarism is given further credence when he sets out to add subtlety to his perceptions. When he smells Wowaran, the scent of yam flowers, he introduces a new abstraction to his life. 'Overpowering' becomes the hallmark by which he compares one scent to another. He can now determine grades of difference. He develops this ability even more when he notices the yam's 'whiteness', thus equipping him with a knowledge of colour. We begin to feel that Nangina had broadened his horizons considerably. A world of discernment and discrimination has opened up to him. In the process he begins to take possession of places and things — i.e. knowledge — in his own right. When he states that Danbamiri, the 'white place' now belongs to him, he is really saying that he has acquired ability to discriminate.

The power of feeling and affection is realized. We know, for instance, that Aborigines today still relate how they feel to various parts of the body. The ears, for example, are said to be the seat of wisdom, since it is through these that knowledge is received. The stomach is considered to be the seat of happiness, pleasure and generosity, while the liver is associated with affection, not the heart. Anger is located in the pancreas, and bones are considered to be the 'foundation' or 'theme' of anything. The theme of any speech is spoken of as the 'bone-that'. A man who is avaricious is someone described as having his 'rectum-large'. When a man fails another, it is said 'my innards, you-took'. And when a man is seen to be acting suspiciously, his liver is said to be 'smiting him'. A disagreement between two men is termed 'words kissing one another', and a man who rests on his laurels is said to 'hold a pillow next to his head'. Finally, a man who gives a wise reply, it is said of him that 'he-his ears — from them answered.'[3] We see how language embraces perceived bodily functions as a way that builds up conceptual images capable of embracing this new power of discrimination and discernment. It is this power that Nangina inaugurated when he smelt the scent of yam blossoms and pronounced them 'overpowering'.

We now enter the realm of dreams and visions. Nangina sees himself walking in a dream. He encounters himself encountering another in the form of the limping yam, presumably a Wandjina like himself, since he catches up with its image in a cave where it has become a painting. This is an important moment in the evolution of Nangina as a spiritual being. Until now his actions have always been conditioned by impulse and affection. He has done things in a relatively unthinking state. Indeed he has so far only partially drawn upon his full intellectual capacities. But now he partakes of a dream condition, the visionary state. He has developed the ability to meditate, and by entering into a state of receptivity he has taught himself how to reflect on his dreams. Already we see a speculative element entering his persona. He is no longer simply a man of action, but has become a seer, a visionary. We know that whatever Nangina experiences in the future he will be able to draw upon that quality of otherness inherent in the contemplative act. Elkin argues that Aborigines are predisposed towards meditation by the quietness and silence of their environment. This, he maintains, encourages a pre-occupation with psychic phenomena which teaches them how to interpret dreams.[4]

Nangina's discussion with the Dreaming hero provokes a mysterious response from the limping yam. The nomenclature "I'm a bushy splitter" implies its individual genus, which Nangina readily agrees to accept as a category, and as a further refinement in his quest for knowledge. From now on there are more than one species of yam in the world. In his dream he has learnt to recognize the symbolic nature of the 'limping yam' as being a way of describing the malformed state of certain yam species. The bushy splitter yam 'limps' into this world by way of the curious nature of its shape. Upon waking Nangina at once wishes to find the yam's cave in which this Dreaming hero has chosen to reside. So he begins a journey in search of the yam cave. When he finds the cave he discovers the Wandjina's imprint on the wall. At this point he feels the need to emulate the workings of the god, and paint more yam images on the space nearby. At once he engages in an act of mimesis, re-creating the image of deity for himself. Art is realized. From out of the immanent place in his heart, the very core of his ideal being, Nangina realizes a complete self-identification with the yam Wandjina. Seer and seen become one, since, in the words of Dante, he 'Who paints a figure, if he cannot be it, cannot draw it.'[5]

We begin to realize that Nangina is no longer the same man who emerged from the spinifex grass at Ngalenga hill. He has become a man of spiritual insight, a man yearning to express the deeper metaphors of reality. Red ochre and pipeclay, the two power colours representing blood and strength, are brought into play. He draws his yams in the image of what he has seen in his vision, none other than the 'limping yam' who describes himself as a 'bushy splitter'. We know by the description that the rock was 'so soft' at this point, a further confirmation that the incident occurred at the time of the Dreaming when the earth was considered to be still malleable. Nangina hurries to complete his task of recreation before it has solidified. When his task is completed, he pronounces the name of the place 'Yalanba' in honour of the Wandjina whom he has helped to make it his home.

Already Nangina has achieved a great deal along the road to self-realization. But until now he has always acted alone. His world has been populated by events, places, principalities and powers. Only he and the Wandjina have been able to enter into some sort of metaphysical dialogue. He has, in a sense, been preoccupied with himself. It is not until he goes for a walk one day and hears a strange noise coming from the river that he realizes the true nature of his solitude. He is like Hai ibn Yaqzin, the hero of the tale which explored the life of a man living a solitary existence on the island of Waq, who was forced to discover everything for himself, since he possessed no teacher (he had been nurtured by a fawn). The arrival of another man on the island occasions long discussions and a new learning experience for Hai. In the process intuitive knowledge and mystical experience are balanced against intellect and reason. Both methods are seen to be complementary ways of acquiring knowledge of truth. The tale of Yaqzin became the prototype for Defoe and the story of Robinson Crusoe.[6] Yaqzin, like Crusoe, did not really begin to learn about truth until he was visited on his island by someone other than himself, a friend and alter ego, a Friday.

The idea that truth can be attained by two means, namely the preparatory and the experiential, finds its echo in the story of

Nangina also. Until he takes a woman to be his wife, Nangina has experienced truth only as the perception of a totally different world. With difficulty is he able to find words to describe how he feels since, in reality, he has no one to talk to. His constant naming of places and things is a reflection of his need to identify these feelings in the absence of another person. Nonetheless, by repeating his actions, he is somehow able to make them into a familiar experience. It is only at this stage that a genuine seeker, in this case Nangina, becomes conscious of truth and of the self. But if he is to progress and become more differentiated, then he must become unconscious of the self and begin to recognize the existence of the other by identifying with someone else. His encounter with Njalbagud in the river represents this moment for him. He sees her as 'beautiful', 'new', indeed the very essence of someone other than himself. The mysterious, passionate encounter between man and women, between opposing realities, is celebrated for the first time. Nangina gazes at the woman with the glittering breasts and pronounces her his. He desires her for herself alone.

Nangina's encounter with his dusky Eve strikes a deep chord. We sense the concord between seer and seen, between these two opposing realities, which in themselves are drawn to the prospect of achieving complete self-identification in one another. To those outside the circle of this abiding encounter, those other women in the stream, Nangina does indeed seem like a devil. For he has chosen to take one of them away, drag her off by the arm and so invest her with an identity in the form of Njalbagud, the 'Woman of the Broken Arm'. She is no longer merely a twittering voice in the river, a non-entity, but his 'boss' woman, his helpmate and equal. Their mutuality is displayed in their adoption of separate roles as hunter and gatherer, and the love and respect they show in the gifts they offer one another. A pile of yams and a morsel of kangaroo fat become an expression of the language of feeling, of caring for someone other than oneself. Moreover Nangina, in his act of offering Njalbagud the kangaroo fat, has shown his preference for companionship over that of his previous solitary life.

Indeed all his actions from this point onward signal his changing role. With Njalbagud he begins to build the rudiments of the first society. All their actions are geared to creating an environment larger than themselves — an environment which intimates a *future*, not just a present. New cooking techniques, presumably the establishment of a bush camp, daily rituals which include hunting and gathering for the benefit of the common hearth, the strengthening of familial bonds and the desire to express these — such are the integers of their newly acquired sociability. Nangina, the lone Wandjina man, has added a new dimension to his existence. He has taken his wife 'home' to Ngalenga hill, there to establish what Crusoe viewed as a 'delightful Cavity' wherein he might feel safe from all the terrors of existential aloneness. And, like Crusoe with his friend Friday, we feel that Nangina had at last found with Njalbagud 'Compleat happiness' insofar as it could be found in a 'sublunary state'.

All our attention is now focused on this family living at Ngalenga. Husband and wife have emerged from their inchoate conditions under earth and in water to find one another at last. Between them they breathe in the same air, and the mystery of fire has been discovered. The four elements of Creation have been identified and drawn together for the first time. The sapiential serpent resides in the cave in the form of a Wandjina painting which Nangina has chosen to recreate. We are conscious that all the ingredients that make up a full physical and spiritual life have now been evolved. We know that the world is a (since the advent of the divine family. Nothing will ever be the same again. Not only have things been accepted in their objective state, but they have also been made subjective by two beings intent on transforming the landscape into one that is both inner and outer. At this point the idea of culture has been fully realized. No more can a solitary being stride across the landscape enjoying something for himself alone. He must learn to share it with all humankind, with nature, and with the spirit-entities that inhabit the upper and lower regions. The world of *maya* or illusion is embraced by the higher world of the Wandjinas and the lower world of the demons. The forces of growth are balanced and harmonized by those of dissolution. In this tripartite universe time does not move in a straight line, from past to present to future, but rather in cycles of growth and decay.

In the wild reaches of the Kimberley we see two people standing on an outcrop and shielding their eyes in order to look upon the rugged emptiness of the world. Their unity is fragile. We sense that they long for something more in order to add a new completeness to their lives. Perhaps they are conscious of the forces of dissolution that dog their footsteps even as they enjoy their freedom. How can they protect themselves from the shadow of death which threatens to engulf them? This is the age-old dilemma in which Nangina and Njalbagud find themselves. It appears that the 'Woman of the Broken Arm' and the 'Man of Darkness' have no other choice but to celebrate their enchantment by binding themselves ever more tightly to the wheel of agony and delight, which itself masquerades as the 'continuous creation' of the world. They must give birth to something which perpetuates what they have so far attained: that knowledge of culture and the art of the pristine spirit which promises to break the shackles of self-hypnotism and the terrible round of rebirth.

We must pause here to contemplate the predicament in which Nangina and Njalbagud find themselves. ho among us has not considered what might happen if we reject the need to recreate ourselves? For the initiated being all opposition, as well as identity, is derived from understanding the essential nature of illusion. So too are wisdom and increase, stability and readiness to assist, compassion and serenity. Such is its power that it can also set us free to contemplate the unity of opposites. Nangina and Njalbagud find themselves embroiled in the task of resolving the union of the 'pairs of opposites' and so entering into a new stage of self-illumination. We can only follow them in their endeavour, watch as they move away from their solitude in order to reproduce themselves in a child whose body is the body of the world.

CHAPTER 12
Exile from the Kingdom

> I shall remain in my place.
> I shall make the cave,
> then I shall go to sleep.
> I am remaining.[1]

According to Aboriginal belief, at least in the northwest, children are not born other than through the intercession of Wandjinas. Women are passive links in the reproductive cycle only, and play no part in conception. This is the preserve of men and their dialogue with the spirits. After world-creation, the Wandjinas left an unlimited supply of spirit-children in waterholes, more specifically in the bodies of fish or other water creatures, such as turtles or freshwater crayfish. Permanent waterholes are the home of all the spirit-children, known as *jilmas*, who await their turn to enter a woman by way of a father's dream.[2]

Numerous myths confirm the link between water, the Wandjinas as water spirits, and their primacy in the act of conception. One myth identifies this event as extending to all nature. We note in passing also the creation of a cave, a Wandjina centre, at the end of a Dream journey which seems to suggest that these shelters also have a practical role to play for those wishing to escape the full force of the monsoon rains. It appears that such *temenoi* or sacred centres are sanctuaries in more ways than one.

Galaru was the first to make nature spirits. He stayed then in his own place: he came this way from the east. Galaru is a stone; he turned himself into a stone. He lives in the water, and sends out spirit-children. He is also the creator of man. He created the emu [a large wingless bird]. Who made the emu? it was Andjalmara. Galaru flashes like lightning. The cave leans outwards, and it is a big cave, in the Dreaming. Who set it up? Galaru set it up, in the Dreaming. He set up Alambuna. He brought it on his shoulder from the south-country and set it up.[3]

Here we see Galaru, a Rainbow Snake and sibling to the Wandjina, identified as the purveyor of spirit-children. He is also a world-creator who makes his own cave, and by implication 'becomes a painting' at the end of his work. But the important issue here is that we see a prefiguration of Nangina's actions before he walked down to a waterhole in his dream. He literally conceived his son while he lay in the swamp grass, watching the spirit-children frolicking in the water. Spirit-children are the offspring of the Wandjina themselves. According to Central Australian belief at least, they are 'born out of their own eternity' (*altjirama nambakala*).[4]

Furthermore, Nangina, after he had asked the spirit-child to identify himself, caught the spirit and placed him on his head. He attached the *jilma* to the seat of his intellect. In other words he carried his 'own eternity' in close proximity to his thoughts, to his aspirations. His dream embodied his desire to perpetuate his acculterated existence beyond his given allotment of years. In this way Nangina had begun to sense the importance of the transmission of metaphysical information 'generation to generation' as Aborigines often remark when they acknowledge the value of tradition. A man cannot quit this earth successfully without bestowing his knowledge on the next generation. This is the basis of all initiatory rites: they ritualize the process of transmission from one generation to the next.

Since Aborigines do not acknowledge physical paternity, the entry of the spirit-child into the mother's womb poses its own problem. Quite often it is accounted for by the entry of the *jilma* through the foot or some other part of the body. In Nangina's case we see him placing the spirit-child on the pubic hair of Njalbagud while she sleeps. The *jilma* then crawls into the mother's womb and the process of quickening begins. It may be that Aborigines are consciously emulating the nativity of kangaroos, only in reverse. It is true, for example, that baby kangaroos are born in a relatively undeveloped state, and are no bigger in length than half a thumb. As soon as they are born, they travel upwards from the birth canal to the pouch, where the teets are located, by crawling through the mother's fur. They then attach themselves to one of the teets and grow to relative maturity outside the womb. At any one time a kangaroo may have infants in its pouch which are at various stages of development, from a tiny homunculus to a fully developed joey. It is likely that since Aborigines are familiar with these events, they have chosen to integrate these into their own belief system. In any event, Njalbagud awakens to find herself in the act of becoming a mother.

The conversaton between Nangina and his wife serves to emphasise their belief in spiritual conception. She dreams of her child drinking from her breasts. The *jilma*, whose real father is the Wandjina, is, in a sense, the implantation of deity in the mother. We are seeing here a prototypal version of the entry of the Holy Spirit into the womb of Mary at the behest of God. From an Aboriginal point of view the immaculate conception *per se* is a gift to all women, not just to the select. All women are capable of — and do — bear offspring that trace their origin back to the spirit. To suggest the uniqueness of the birth of Jesus Christ in the light of this knowledge is to dismiss mythogenic reality and its close identification with the concept of virgin birth. Among Aborigines it seems that all women are virgins, just as all women are mothers. The fact that Njalbagud places the umbilical cord around her neck after the child's birth signifies that she too recognizes the navel's identity with the womb as the feminine centre of life, from which the universe is nourished.

In the following sequence describing the child's infancy and youth, we are witnessing exemplarism in the form of various cultural practices. The child learns to walk, play games, travel on his mother's shoulder in a particular way, and begins to identify with the values of the first parents. Wulawodei, though never as clearly identified as Nangina or Njalbagud, is nonetheless important to the myth. He, after all, is the one who survives, who carries the filial message of world-birth and culture beyond the

153

Dreaming into human consciousness. He is the true Messenger, the Dreaming hero who presents humankind with a record of these divine events. We watch his progress from infant to independent being, knowing that he will eventually take over the mantle of avatar when his father 'becomes a painting.'

But it is the advent of a bushfire which changes the lives of the first family for good. On the outbreak of the fire they are drawn into contact with others — with other 'first families', so to speak. The practice of burning off country in order to encourage new growth, which animals like kangaroos particularly enjoy, is a very ancient custom. It is also common as a way of forcing game to flee in the direction of an ambush. That Nangina sees the billowing smoke and decides to investigate suggests that he has accepted the need to enter into a relationship with others. This is confirmed when he presents himself at the camp of this unknown group of tribesmen; he sits some distance away in accordance with good manners — until he is invited to join them by the fire.

When night falls we find ourselves present at a corroboree, or ceremonial dance. The tribesmen entertain their visitor to the sound of clapsticks and didgeridoo (a type of long wooden horn). We see them stamp their feet on the ground to the beat of the music. Nangina responds by singing a song describing his totemic home at Ngalenga. In this song he mentions an 'invisible rope', what is known as a *biju* or aerial rope. We realize at once that Nangina has already acquired the mystic powers of a *barnmunji* or witch doctor. For this rope is used exclusively by doctor men to fly through the air and render themselves invisible. Therefore we know that he has undergone ritual cleansing, and has been reborn as a *barnmunji*. His insides have been removed and replaced with magical quartz crystals known as *gedji*. These crystals are said to have fallen to earth from above in the form of 'solidified light', and in so doing reflect a scintilla of divine attributes now present in the *barnmunji*. Nangina has acquired occult powers in the presence of the Wandjina painting back at Ngalenga. He has become a custodian of mystical lore essential to the magical transformation of ordinary events into those which intimate the presence of the Wandjina on earth.[5] He now embodies not only the hunter, husband, and father, but the priest as well. He has become a 'man of high degree' as Elkin so eloquently describes.

His performance is received by the tribesmen in an aura of duplicity and deceit. Lies and the false expression of sentiment pervade the evening. They speak with forked tongues. Nangina is oblivious to the danger that surrounds him. That he is a solitary man with no patrilinial affiliations makes him different from the men seated nearby. However much he might wish to entertain or instruct them, his singularity separates him from the clan orientation of the others. When they do decide to attack him, it is because he represents someone alien, being a non-tribal member. His uniqueness singles him out for destruction since it is this that threatens the validity of their collective identity. Like any demigogue, Nangina represents the power of the individual over the collective, a situation that is anathema to Aborigines who are at pains to emphasise the pre-eminence of the elders in tribal government. Aboriginal society is gerontocratic, with numerous checks and balances built into it in to protect the authority of the elders.

What follows is a bitter confrontation between the individual and the collective. Nangina is set upon by the tribesmen who desire his death. The outcome favours Nangina, who manages to kill many men. His manliness is glorified. He becomes a warrior in spite of himself. He calls out to his wife to bring him his weapons, then he goes on a rampage, spearing men at random. It is as though he had become a victim of blood-lust, unable to quell the destructive emotions which now possess him. We sense at this point that Nangina has changed. He is no longer the innocent man who has wandered the land since the time of the Dreaming, untrammelled by pain or anguish. Until now he has been favoured, a part god, someone who valued his independence and his freedom. By entering the tribesmen's camp he had allowed himself to be seduced by the prospect of a companionship different from that offered by his family. In the act of wishing to fulfill what he felt was his lack, Nangina had inadvertently politicized his being. No more could he remain aloof from the affairs of men. By killing these tribesmen he had committed a felony which made him one of them. All the cares of the world were now on his shoulders. He had committed a crime which would remain with him for the rest of his days.

This becomes a turning-point in Nangina's life. From now on he must carry with him a sense of guilt. Although it is never mentioned in the narrative, we sense that more than anything Nangina desires to purge himself of this crime, expunge its memory forever. He calls for his firestick and attempts to set ablaze the lower world of men. He sweeps across the country, setting the grasslands alight. Soon a mighty conflagration consumes the earth. The only secure place left is the sacred centre of Ngalenga, his spiritual birthplace and home, the place where the Wandjina resides. It is as if Nangina wanted to erase everything from the earth and begin the process of Creation anew. Ultimately the nature of his anguish lies in the fact that he has revealed too much of what he knows to those 'unnamed' tribesmen, in the hope of winning their respect. They have deceived him into telling them what he knows so that they might gain power over him. His cry, "Where's my son?" echoes the intensity of his anguish. He knows that his own youth has finally disappeared in this brazen act of genocide. Though, on the surface, it may appear that it was not his fault that he had been attacked, Nangina's destiny was always going to be linked to some principial act of wrongdoing, in order that he too might embrace fully the human predicament. His destiny was not to remain untouched by the conflict and resolution inherent in the 'pairs of opposites' which governed his world-birth. Nangina had to 'become' man before he could take on fully the trappings of a Wandjina.

The return of the first family to the cave at Ngalenga completes the uroboric cycle of return. In an attempt to recontruct the past in all its pristine grandeur, they return to the cave where the yams are stored. What they do not realize, however, is that Ngalenga is the only place left in the world not damaged by the great fire. Its very perfection sets it apart, and makes it an object of pilgrimage for others. No longer can Nangina remain isolated from the world. People now come searching for him in their attempt to rectify the cosmic diremption caused by him. But before they can confront Nangina, the warriors realize that they must bury their dead in accordance with their beliefs.

Cave burial is usually reserved for the bones of the deceased after they have undergone tree-stage burial. Furthermore, as it has been mentioned earlier, Wandjina cave burial is reserved for important elders. In contrast women are buried in the ground. Another Wandjina myth celebrating the journey and death of Waningiyala details the procedure of tree-stage burial. Here is an excerpt:

> After his sons went hunting, he went and dug up yellow clay. "I want to paint myself," he said.
>
> He lay down then, and his children came to him in the afternoon and gave him kangaroo to eat. Waningiyala pounded the meat and mixed it with water. He ate it and was satisfied. Then he got water and bathed himself. He lay down and dipped his foot in the water and died. They made a tree-platform for his body and laid him on top.
>
> "We will lay him on top, and we will be able to see him for a good while," they said.
>
> So they lifted him up onto the platform and jammed his leg with the wattle tree so that he would not fall down.
>
> "Then we can look at him," they said.
>
> Now he lies there on top. He turns around. In the first watch, he is lying towards the east [dawn]. Then he turns to the west [sunset] and pillows himself till near daylight. He turns and pillows southwest till sunrise, and then dips himself in the water to the southwest.[6]

While this myth explores burial practices, we note in passing that in the narrative the Milky Way is symbolized, along with its movement across the sky at night. According to Coate, the Milky Way is the tree-platform on which the corpse of a dead person is placed until the inquest has been held to determine the cause of death, and until the bones are freed from the flesh. The bones are brought down in order to become the centrepiece of a 'delayed' mourning ritual. They are then disposed of, usually in a Wandjina cave or rock shelter. In this myth the one who died (after dipping his foot in the water) was Walanganda, the Rainbow Serpent, who was transported to the sky on his special burial tree-platform, the Milky Way. This platform slowly turns according to the watches of the night — that is, from an easterly direction to the southwest. At sunrise it dips down into the waters, just as Walanganda did at the time of the Dreaming when he dipped his feet in the water when he was dying. As a footnote Coate explains that Walanganda was responsible for certain food laws, and the creation of water. When he returned to the sky Walanganda created the 'water' in the Milky Way (ie. its stream-like effect). 'He lies down there, his footprint visible. He instructed the Wandjina to go to the caves on earth and look after the rain. He hangs up the clouds and sends the living creatures.'[7]

In this context we see how burial practice reflects that of a celestial death, in this case the Rainbow Serpent's. Man consciously emulates the Sky Hero in everything he does. We note also that the Wandjina are seen as subordinate to the Rainbow Serpent, Walanganda (who is often associated with the two pointer stars in the Southern Cross). They are both principial beings associated with manifestation since they 'make' the world. However it is clear that some hierarchy does exist. The unmanifest principle is known as Ngadjaia, the Supreme Being, who stands above them both.[8]

The tribesmen return to the Wandjina cave with the bones of their dead. They also transport them to another Wandjina cave, so that we are made aware that the world has 'expanded' considerably since Nangina first emerged from the spinifex grass at Ngalenga. Meanwhile Wulawodei has grown into a man, and learnt the ways of his father. Nangina too is growing old. Nonetheless, though his feet are unsteady and his hair is grey, he still retains his memories. But these trouble him. He is deeply afflicted by the pain of his actions all those years ago. In the end he knows he must make peace with his assailants before he dies, otherwise his spirit will not be at rest.

The Man of Darkness is aware that he is dying. He is conscious that he has entered the phase known as 'dying round the holy power'. As the 'priest of fire' he knows he must sit down with his foes and try to resolve their differences together. In the constant battle for cosmic supremacy between the spirits and anti-spirits, Nangina is aware of the need to patch up their differences, at least so that the way of ritual action might be preserved. This, and this alone will ensure the future of the world. In a sense he is the Dying King, ready to lay down his life in the interest of cosmic harmony. We are conscious that his final journey to the camp of his foes to attend a corroboree represents his last act of contrition. Nangina is ready now to unburden himself of all that he knows so that the way of ritual action might come into the possession of others.

The last act of the drama involves the final resolution of opposites. It is a moment of poignancy for both parties. The tribesmen listen to Nangina in silence. Though they feel sorry for him, they also recognize him to be the bearer of sacred knowledge. For the time being he is bound to them, and is under their protection just so long as he retains power over them. But when he has revealed all he knows about the secret workings of nature, and passed on to them the tenets of sacred law, he knows it will be a signal for them to fall upon him and exact their revenge. He knows also that he must allow this to happen if the 'sins of the father' are not to be inherited by his son. We sense that Nangina has chosen to become the first sacrifice so that men will remember him for all time. As he remarked, "I will be famous." By his actions Nangina's heroic status is confirmed. In allowing himself to be killed he has entered the company of Dreaming heroes and 'become a painting' himself. "Isn't that your place?" the tribesmen asked. "What place?" he answered, knowing that they had discovered his Wandjina death-place, his spirit platform in which his essence would remain for evermore, a place of pilgrimage for those that came after him.

Meanwhile Ngalenga is to become like Sammeda hill, a place sacred to the Jains of India, where numerous saints and sages were said to have attained enlightenment. Like the Lord Parsva, who had passed on to his final liberation and allowed his corpse to repose on the summit of this hill, Ngalenga does the same. As the once youthful 'prince of fire' his corpse is laid to rest on its tree-platform, there to turn around in accordance with the precession of the stars. His spirit watches the sun rising and setting into the dim reaches of time, untrammelled by the contrictions of physical existence. As the first man his apotheosis as a god, as a Wandjina, is assured. His discoveries of food and fire place him among a select pantheon of spirit-beings. That he has also acquired occultic knowledge and bestowed it upon men places him in a unique category of his own. Who but he has discovered Wunbala, the 'rear side of the hill', the very essence of things, and returned to tell the story?

The myth of Nangina draws to a close. We are left contemplating the birth of the first man and his apotheosis within ourselves. All his actions and discoveries, his encounters with the world of nature and of men, are redolent with the scent of yam flowers. They are, in his words, *wowaran*, overpowering. Nangina has given us insight into the way the world begins. He has shown us how consciousness emerges from the stygean depths of unbridled existence and begins to mould it into concrete forms. We see the individual put in touch with the totality of nature for the first time, and how his perceptions radiate in all directions as they begin to grapple with its enormity. Nangina is an extremely gifted spirit-being because he recognizes in nature the source of life and energy. He has seen the fearsome life that lies at the heart of nature, and bent it to his will. The knowledge of fire and the transformative energy of food made him into a superman. No man is able to bring him down, not even the anti-spirits masquerading as tribesmen. He 'slips' from their grasp even as they attempt to pinion him.

Nangina lives in us all. He is the principial being within us who enters into the world of nature and extracts from it its fiery essence. In the act of naming things he identifies himself with the destiny of all things. They become his cohorts. Grass, birds, animals, mountains and rivers — these have emerged from the earth just as he has. As a Wandjina he has given them life and form because of his link with the fructive waters of the monsoon rains. His cloud-like face looms on the horizon as it does in caves and rock shelters, a mountain of cumulus-bearing rain reflected in his gaze. He is Ngadjaia's representative here on earth. He gives us law and knowledge. Every spring and waterhole bears countless numbers of his spirit-children who await their opportunity to enter into the dreams of men, and so into the world. We glory in his eternal existence as we glory in that of Njalbagud and Wulawodei. They are the first family who conceived us as one of their own.

This is the message from the Wandjinas of the Kimberley. Unlike any other spirit-entity in Australia, they occupy a special space in our imagination. They seem so much larger than the space devoted to their worship in the isolated rock shelters and caves of the northwest. We are captivated by their presence because, in a way, they reflect the earliest image we have of deity. Their mouthless visages embody principial identity and the physical manifestation of the invisible forces governing the conduct of nature itself. No man can undestand these; he can only revere them and celebrate them by way of ritual action. The Wandjinas whose paintings are the very soul of earth wisdom, continue to present their faces to the world in the hope that we too will embrace their idea of unity.

If they have any underlying message it must be that the 'pairs of opposites' which hang around our necks like Njalbagud's umbilical cord, that remnant of our birth, can be made to transmit anew its life-giving properties. Indeed the Wandjinas intimate the supreme, unchanging, all-pervading source and end of being which makes up the substratum of life, and the consciousness of all existing forms. In their majesty these spirit-beings speak to us of a time when the world was, is, and will be ever new. Their aeternality pervades the very ground upon which we walk. If we accept their reality as abiding earth spirits, then already we are making the first steps towards a raprochement with nature. This, surely, is the commitment the Wandjina are calling upon us to make: they want us to recognize the beginning of a process whereby the Dreaming becomes a reality for all men, not just for Aborigines.

Conclusion

Myth is the supreme metaphysical language. No other language expresses so well the complexity surrounding the mystery of the earth's origins. Science may be able to explain such events in terms of empirical evidence, but it cannot evoke these events in terms of their significance. Nor do meaning and explanation always coincide when it comes to understanding the essential nature of custom and belief. Only *mythos* has the power to overcome the prosaic, and make old beauties seem like new again. Our hunger for myth is none other than a hankering for an intoxicant that will continue to stimulate and vivify us long after we have accepted the facts. More than anything we desire to partake of a spiritual food which will sustain us when we are feeling most vulnerable. It is in the myth that we allow ourselves to be ravished quite out of ourselves. In so doing we find ourselves so deeply altered that we begin to fall into a world where all is *signification*, out of a world where all is simply sign.

A culture that has lost this hunger is in itself burnt out. It has lost the ability to transform itself through an act of ritual transcendence. Critical thought destroys the link between the godly powers and ourselves which was formerly woven for us by our sacraments and dogmas. As Nietzsche remarked, myth is a kind or style of thinking. It imparts an idea of the universe in a sequence of events, actions, and sufferings. Looking into it is like gazing into a mirror or fountain full of hints and prophesies. Myth is the sole and spontaneous image of life itself n its overflowing harmony and mutually hostile contraries. Therein lies its inexhaustible power.

In this book we have explored the worlds of three important spirit-beings — the dog-man Ankotarinja, the Rainbow Serpent Julungul, and Nangina Wandjina, the first man. The archaic splendor of the events surrounding their lives are now a part of our own. We have emerged from the earth at Ankota, danced before the figure of Julungul by Muruwul waterhole, and set fire

163

Conclusion

to the grasslands near Ngalenga in a fit of despair. We have taken part in the epical masquerade and distant interfusion of all these spirit-beings as they enacted their mutual opposition and appeasement. All the contraries of Creation have been evoked within ourselves, showering forth upon us the knowledge that the earth is forever embraced by its *invisible* counterpart, those forces that activate nature itself. Some might see these forces as originating in the earth, and therefore of a lesser order. Others might regard them as purely metaphysical, and therefore partaking of another reality altogether. Whatever one's views, it is clear that *mythos* contains a dimension not present in ordinary narrative, history, or analysis.

In an age which has forsaken mythogenesis because of its links with archaic thinking, we have yet to find an appropriate form of metaphysical enquiry to counteract logical thought. Nonetheless myth does allow thought the opportunity to bridge the gap between perception and observation, recognition and acceptance. Through myth, what we encounter with our senses can be amended by what we feel. By cultivating this 'sixth sense' early man sought to reconcile himself with those powerful forces which governed nature in a way that provided acceptable answers to the great questions of life. The myth was the vehicle by which he entered into a state of subjectivity in relation to his origins. No longer did he stand outside the process; the myth allowed him to continually recreate events from the past in a ritually satisfying way. Myth became a method by which his 'inner sense' could be constructively channelled.

At the onset of this journey into myth we tried to invoke the idea that each myth was its own mask. Since the word 'mask' is derived from the idea of the net or snare, it is easy to see how the myth really works. Rather than revealing information in the course of its enactment, the myth in fact ensnares the observer, and so draws him into its web of truth. It does not stand alone as a narrative object; instead the myth acts in accordance with mysterious rules which govern the conduct of concealment. These rules have been devised to ensure that the 'pairs of

Conclusion

opposites' (ie. inherent duality) will ultimately appear to be unified, if in a non-rational way. Nor can the observer extract this unity from the myth in any concrete fashion. He is left with a series of paradoxical and often anthithetical events which in themselves conceal the unity he strives to attain within himself. Like the Grail, he must continue to search for this mysterious unity, conscious that it will remain forever outside his grasp.

Ankotarinja, Julungul, the Wauwalak Sisters, and Nangina embody certain archetypal realities. They are neither heroes nor gods, spirit-entities nor demons. Their presence within the myth defies description or characterization since they partake of a potentiality that is both multifarious and non-existent. No man has actually seen Julungul or Ankotarinja, but this is not to say that they are not always present, if not 'in the flesh,' then at least as emanation. Indeed who has not felt the presence of something 'wholly other' in a sacred place as Otto so succinctly describes?[1] Like stored up electricity, this hidden force in nature discharges its energy on anyone who happens to come near. Incalculable and arbitrary, such a presence can be both wilful and capricious, thereby conjuring up a feeling of dread. Mythic spirit-beings, whether they are Aboriginal, Greek, Vedic, Amerindian or African, will always infer their presence in a sanctuary, and thus infer the nature of their persona in their individual form of 'wrath' (*orgé*). This wrath is normally associated with the 'wrath of God', but it is equally applicable as a description of mythogenic presence.

Malinowski regarded myth not as explanation put forward to satisfy scientific curiosity, but as the re-arising of a primordial reality in narrative form:

> The myth in a primitive society, ie. in its original living form, is not a mere tale told but a reality lived. It is not in the nature of an invention such as we read in our novels today, but living reality, believed to have occurred in primordial times and to be influencing ever afterwards the world and the destinies of men... These stories are not kept alive by vain curiosity, neither as tales that have been invented nor again as tales that are true. For the natives on the

Conclusion

contrary, they are an assertion of an original, greater, and more important reality through which the present life, fate and work of mankind are governed, and the knowledge of which provides men on the one hand with motives for ritual and moral acts, on the other with directions for their performance.[2]

Since myth's principal role is to set up some precedent as an ideal, and as a guarantee of the continuence of that ideal, its task is not to 'explain' but to lay the foundation upon which primary principles may forever rest. The early Greek philosophers regarded these primary principles as 'boundless' (*apaeron*), and therefore substances or states that never age, can never be surpassed, and which produce everything always. Water or fire may be considered as examples of such substances. Like myth, they form the ground or foundation of the world, since everything rests on them. They represent the principle to which everything individual and particular goes back, and out of which it is made. These in themselves remain ageless, inexhaustible, invincible in timeless primordality, existing in a past that proves to be imperishable because of its eternally repeated rebirths.

Aboriginal myths stimulate us precisely because they are grounded in these principles. At no time do we sense that extraneous elements have crept into the mythologem itself. Fire, earth, air, water, birth, war, apotheosis, magical transformation, such are the pillars which support mythical structure, even for Aborigines. They exist outside time and only superficially in the realm of events. We are drawn into an autochthonous world where a divine act becomes synonymous with regionality and ritual. In listening to a myth we are able to find our way back to primeval times. Suddenly, without any digression or searching on our part, without any studious investigation or effort, we become immersed in the primordality that is our perennial concern, in the midst of those principles once more. We experience our own origin as a developed spiritual being thanks to this kind of identification, and so become a world-unit, a microcosmos in the totality of the myth itself.

Conclusion

We cannot help but identify with the likes of, say, Ankotarinja or Nangina. These mythic heroes announce to us our concerns, our preoccupation with the questions of 'Why?' or 'When?' The philosopher may try to pierce through the world of appearances in order to say what 'really is' in this context; but we who listen to the myth prefer to step back into primordality in order to hear what 'really was'. There is satisfaction in hearing how things 'really were' in the context of truth, rather than knowing how things 'really are' in the context of fact. Perhaps this is because we long to actually experience truth as a principle, instead of encountering it as an intellectual or sensual reality only. The myth provides us with a way of descending into the depths of these principles, so that they invest us with all their metaphysical hues. In turn we are able to see ourselves as part of a fraternity whose essential role is to resolve the hiatus between opposing realities, those 'pairs of opposites' wherein fulfilment ultimately resides.

We have a significant role to play in the mythogenic process. None more so than when we translate a mythological value into an act when we participate in a ceremony or ritual. By doing so, we are able to transcend the *mundus saecularus* which has so distorted our contemporary world. Eliade maintains that, in the modern context at least, we have become non-religious, and therefore have denied ourselves the possibility of transcendence.[3] We regard urselves as solely the agent and subject of history, and so refuse all appeal to the transcendent. We accept no model for humanity outside the human condition as it is paraded in various historical situations. In other words, we *make ourselves*, and we only do so successfully in proportion to how much we desacralize ourselves and the world. If we were only to admit it, we would recognize that the sacred is the prime obstacle to our quest for freedom. The cry of Thamus, as related by Plutarch: "Great Pan is dead," echoes down through the ages as the obituary pronounced over the death of all gods, mythic or otherwise.[4]

By returning to the most ancient myths, such as those of the

Conclusion

Aborigines, it may be possible to revive Pan before it is too late. Many great scholars like Walter Otto, Karl Kerényi, Mircea Eleade, Heinrich Zimmer, Ananda Coomaraswamy and others have preceded us in this endeavour, and have managed to revive interest in the mythogenic process. These men sought to highlight the numinosity of myth over its folkloric elements. But even they were forced to combat the Kantian view that 'God was not an external substance but only a moral condition within us.' Freud, and to a certain extent Jung ('all archetypes are manifestations of processes in the collective unconscious'), tried to prove that religion was the indirect result of traumatic accident out of which humankind invented a 'god' to meet his 'needs'. So that the genuine theist always found himself being condemned for his lack of objectivity when it came to the study of myths. Because he worked from 'inside', and rejected the psychological and anthropological approach to religion, he was seen to have disregarded the rules of scholasticism and science. Their methods linked them with the pre-Socratic philosophers of the past, and so with a desire to underline essence rather than appearance.

The greatest challenge of our time is to regain for ourselves the patrimony of ancient belief which lies out there in the sub-soil of myth. Where else but in the creekbed at Ankota or in the cave at Ngalenga can we begin to reclaim our inheritance? There, and only there will we find what it is we are looking for — that contact with first principles and the capacity for 'pristine recognition' which were once ours by birthright. Only these have the power to sustain us as we travel through the world of appearances, and grapple with those irreconcilable opposites on the plane of manifestation. Our commitment must be to re-establish the imminence of the momentary god as it intuitively moves within the soul. Ankotarinja's naked encounter with himself in the pool reflects a primary encounter with the numinous, and its reality to us as an archetype. It is this act — the act of self-reflection — that draws us into complicity with mythic heroes. We begin to refashion ourselves *in their image* rather than remain condemned to the restricted carapace of our own self-image. In this lies the full revelation of otherness so inherent in the mythogenic process.

The truth is that which confronts humankind in epiphanies is not a reality which is completely unrecognizable and imperceptible, affecting only the soul which has turned its back on the world, but rather acts upon the world itself as a divine form, as a plenitude of divine configurations. Myths represent primary appearances which stand at the beginning of all the more profound human activities and endeavours. They have the power to transform the individual into a community, and go on to leave their mark on the creations of all the basic forms of human existence. As Otto remarked, 'The greatest creative force is that which succeeds in giving form to human life itself.'[5] In this sense *mythos* weaves its magical spell about the imagination of men, at once concealing and revealing the great occurrences of the earth and the universe. It facilitates a union and interaction with deity, with the transforming power of the spirit-beings themselves.

This is not to say that Ankotarinja, Julungul or Nangina offer up more than their prototypal presence. We cannot look to them to provide us with a structure for living, since this is not their role. While Aborigines might look to them as ritual models, at no time do we see them identifying with these spirit-beings as exemplars in the way that Christians might identify with Christ, or Muslims with Muhammed. Indeed, for Aborigines, ritual activity allows them their *only* point of contact with their Dreaming heroes. Outside of this activity they see them as separate from themselves, possessing a theistic personality which precludes exemplarism altogether. They are not 'gods come down to earth' in human form, but spirit-entities who remain confined to the celestial condition from which they first emerged. This makes a mythic hero somewhat different from an avatar, although it has to be conceded that they do embody avataric tendencies on occasions.

To attempt to identify with a spirit-being is perhaps a most

Conclusion

difficult endeavour. We have been educated in an atmosphere of piety to believe that our destiny is linked to that of a 'God come down to earth'. The idea of entering into a ritual relationship with a mythic hero in order to perform a rite-of-passage seems vaguely demeaning when compared with the spiritual benefits that are said to flow from attending church or mosque. It is inconceivable to think that there may be other, less tangible benefits that could flow from acting out a mythic event. Yet indigenous peoples readily identify with a feeling of otherness that flows forth from such an enactment. Popular expression often identifies this feeling with trance-states and shamanism, but its real nature is closer to that of the Greek word, *mystikos*, meaning an experience derived from participation 'in the mysteries'. Thus a man in the embrace of ritual activity is able to momentarily *transform himself* and become the mythic hero. For indigenous peoples like the Aborigines exemplarism can only happen inside ritual activity, not outside it as it does for Christians or Buddhists. This makes the enactment of a mythic event through ritual tantamount to engaging in an act of prescience, whereby the individual or group see themselves identifying with sacred events as a manifestation of the Dreaming itself.

Mythic activity is not primarily the basis for ethical or social activity. It exists outside these, preferring to teach by way of transformation rather than interpretation. The myth cannot be separated from its rituals or songs, since these represent the 'bones' that support the narrative. In analysing the universal significance of the three myths contained herein we have in no way uncovered every aspect of their meaning. Meaning is not the property of myth anyway, but rather the individual. Only he or she can explore its ramifications as they affect the individual soul. What becomes ours when we encounter a living myth and its concommittant rituals is the feeling that we have participated in an epiphany capable of restoring us, for a short while at least, to a state of primordial innocence. Hopefully the three myths explored herein have helped to highlight how this state is

Conclusion

achieved in the context of Aboriginal culture and belief.

More importantly, perhaps, we need to ask ourselves whether there is room for a renewal of the mythogenic process in modern life. While we might have 'modern myths' to go by, it must be emphasised that these are not real myths as such. They have no power of transformation. Instead they rely on an emotional consensus for their survival (viz. George Washington's refusal to tell a lie after cutting down the apple tree, or Custer's last stand as an embodiment of ethnocentric, Protestant virtues). True myths do not operate on the plane of human values. Their survival is determined by an alliance between our need to reach beyond ourselves — ie. to allow ourselves to be transformed — and that of the powers of nature to meet us half way. True myth derives its integrity from a blend of human cognition, earth wisdom, and metaphysical perambulation. The spiritual journey becomes the essence of myth insofar as such a journey prefigures that which humanity finds itself perpetually engaged in since the beginning of consciousness.

Does the myth offer us anything today? Is there room left in our lives for the sanctification of objective being by way of ritual activity? This is the question we set out to answer at the beginning of this book. Mytho-consciousness still exists among indigenous peoples throughout the world even as they struggle to come to terms with the modern condition. Their solid comprehension of their role within nature as bearers of consciousness, along with other living creatures, places them in a unique position to teach us how to experience the mythogenic process. Alone among peoples they understand what it is to draw comfort from an event that occurs in nature which is itself an echo of a primordial event that occurs 'in heaven'. They teach us to revere the mythogenic process as a timeless record of Creation, and a bearer of numinous detail that is impossible to convey in any other form. Like a spider's web, *mythos* ensnares their imagination with an all but invisible thread woven from the gossamer of celestial events; and these arguably will sustain them long after the illusory nature of the contemporary world

171

has run its course.

So we have to ask whether we wish to subject ourselves to the mythogenic process once more in the interest of our overall wellbeing. If, for example, we wish to draw upon the deep reservoir of spirit lying in the Australian landscape, then we must be prepared to surrender ourselves to the embrace of its Dreaming heroes. It is not impossible to enter into the spirit of Ankotarinja or Nangina, the Rainbow Serpent or the Wauwalak Sisters, just as the Aborigines have done for upwards of 50,000 years. It may be that they can teach us how to re-awaken our mythic sensibility and begin the process of spiritual renewal. By evoking Dreaming events we will be able to restore a sense of harmony and balance to our behaviour when it comes to manipulating the environment. Perhaps Nangina and Ankotarinja might be our last bulwark against the final denudation of the planet.

How this can be achieved remains in the area of conjecture. With the active co-operation of indigenous peoples we can still learn how to participate in the mythogenic process. It is they who can teach us, who can reveal to us its esoteric aspects that are so important to mythic understanding. It is not too late to acquire a taste for mytho-history so long as we can be sure that our instruction is derived from men of knowledge. These men hold the key to a rapprochement between the world of things and that of celestial events. They know how to bridge the gap between the temporal and the eternal simply because they are well versed in those hieratic methods of discourse which have been handed down to them throughout the ages. Their knowledge is the knowledge that remained in the world in the wake of the Dreaming heroes. What they know is derived from mythic reality, and can only be handed on to those who are prepared to accept its message in the proper spirit. We must ask them to help us to participate in this reality before it is too late.

And finally, we must learn to accept mythic heroes as manifestations of numinous forces within nature. They are far more than 'earth spirits'; but rather they are the incarnation of

172

Conclusion

theophanic events. The Wandjinas on the walls of Kimberley caves are perhaps the descendants of the oldest icons known to man. We must learn to revere them as a part of our common human ancestry, indeed as a part of our common striving towards consciousness. This is what the language of myth teaches us. No longer do we find ourselves, like Ankotarinja, burdened by a *tnatantja* that we cannot carry on our heads; or like Julungul, unable to digest what is most sacred in the world; or Nangina, ready to forfeit his life in order to assuage cosmic diremption. Instead we become World Tree, *maraiin* object, and initiatory victim all in one. In us the 'pairs of opposites' can be resolved, the Many made One again. For we are heirs to a great legacy — that of knowing how, when, and why we were born, if only in the form of mythopoeic knowledge. It is this knowledge that will ensure our survival, just as it has contributed to the survival of peoples in the past.

It should be left to one of the tribal elders of the Worora people to explain the significance of myth for us all. Sam Woolagoodjah, now deceased, was an eloquent spokesman for his people. At a time when their future seemed most under threat, he alone stood firm against the encroachment of the modern world, and the values of spiritual diminishment that it embodied. He explained it this way:

> Dreaming,
> The first ones lived, those of long ago.
> They were the Wandjinas —
> Like this one here, Namalee.
> The first ones, those days,
> Shifted from place to place,
> In the Dreaming before the floods came.
> Bird Wandjinas, crab Wandjinas
> Carried the big rocks.
> They threw them into deep water,
> Then piled them on the land.
>
> Other Wandjinas —
> All kinds —

Conclusion

She the rock python,
He the kangaroo,
They changed it.
They struggled with the rocks,
They dug the rivers.
They were the Wandjinas. They talk
With us at some places they have marked.

Where the sun climbs, over the hills
And the river they came,
And they are with us in the land.
We remember how they fought
Each other at those places they marked —
It is Dreaming there.

Some Wandjinas went under the land,
They came to stay in the caves
And there we can see them.
Grown men listen to their Wandjinas.
Long ago, at another time,
These Wandjinas changed the bad ones
Into rocks
And the spring we always drink from.
These places hold our spirits,
These Ungud places of the Wandjinas.
There a man learns
Who his child really is:
Its spirit comes when he is dreaming
And tells him its name.
Then the man has been given his child:
It has its own name
Beside the land-name of its father...[6]

According to Sam Woolagoodja, in the act of listening to the
Wandjinas, all men have the possibility of entering into a mythic
state and becoming whole again. It seems that the gift of
tongues, mythical or otherwise, resides within us.

CHAPTER NOTES
Part I: View from Ankota

Chapter 2
1. T.G.H. Strehlow. *Ankotarinja, an Aranda Myth*. Oceania 4: 1933-4, pp187-200.
2. T.G.H. Strehlow. *Aranda Traditions*, Melbourne University Press, 1947.
3. James G. Cowan. *The Aborigine Tradition*. Element Books, 1992. p. 46.
4. *Ibid*. AT.
5. Walter F. Otto. Quoted in Karl Kerényi's *Hermes, Guide of Souls*, Spring Publications, 1976.
6. *Ibid*. AAM.
7. Max Muller, *The Philosophy of Mythology*, appended to *Introduction to the Science of Religion*. London 1873.
8. *Ibid*. AAM. Included in Strehlow's rendition is the original in the Aranda language.

Chapter 3
1. Geber, 'Summa perfectionis', *De alchemia*. Quoted in C.G. Jung's *Alchemical Studies*, Volume 13. Routledge & Kegan Paul.
2. Rg Veda, X. 88. 6. Quoted in Ananda Coomaraswamy's article *Angle and Titan: an Essay on Vedic Ontology*. Museum of Fine Arts, Boston.
3. Wallace Budge, *The Book of the Dead*.
4. Gerard Dorn, *Speculativa philosophia*, Quoted in C.G. Jung's *Alchemical Studies*.
5. Pabhamananda and Isherwood, *The Song of God*.
6. Ananda Coomaraswamy, *The Inverted Tree*. Quarterly Journal of the Mythic Society (Bangalore) XXIX (1938-9).
7. Ananda Coomaraswamy, *Symblegades*. In 'Selected Papers' Vol. 1 Bollingen series 89, 1977.
8. T.G.H. Strehlow, *Aranda Traditions*.
9. Dieterich, A. Quoted in C.G. Jung's *Symbols of Transformation*. Routledge & Kegan Paul, 1967.

Chapter 4
1. Coomaraswamy A.K. *'Akimcanna; Self-naughting'*, New Indian Antiquary, Vol III. Bombay 1940.
2. Ruland, Martin. *A Lexicon of Alchemy*. London 1892.
3. Frazer J.G. *The Golden Bough*, MacMillan 1978.
4. Spencer Gillan. *The Aranda*, Vol 1.
5. Wallace Budge. *The Mummy*.
6. Coomaraswamy, A.K. *Angel and Titan*.
7. *Ibid*. A & T.
8. Coomaraswamy, A.K. *Sir Garwain and the Green Knight: Indra and Namuci*. Speculum 19, (1944).
9. Rumi, Mevlana Jalaluddin. *Where Two Oceans Meet. A Selection of Odes from the Divan of Shems of Tabriz*. Translated by James C. Cowan. Element Books 1992.

Part II: By Muruwul Waterhole

Chapter 5
1. Layard, John, *Stone Men of Malekula*. Vao: London, 1942.
2. Zimmer, Heinrich. *The Kingdom and the Corpse*. Meridian Books, 1960
3. Berndt, R.M. Kunapipi, Cheshire.
4. Berndt, R.M. *Djanggawul*, Routledge & Kegan Paul.
5. Warner, L. *A Black Civilization*. New York and London, 1937.
6. Coomaraswamy, A.K. *Angel and Titan*.
7. Neumann, Eric. *The Great Mother*. Routledge & Kegan Paul, 1955.

Chapter 6
1. The entire Wauwalak myth is made up of a combination of material derived from R.M. Berndt's *Kunapipi* and Roland Robinson's *Aboriginal Myths and Legends* (Sun Books, 1977). Robinson called the Great Snake 'Wittee' which he considered to be male. This is not inconsistent with Berndt's version, since he acknowledges the dual sexuality of Julungul, both in the context of the 'male' snakes of *jiritja* moiety in the waterhole, as well as her husband who is also known as 'Julungul'. The point is that Julungul is bisexual, as was mentioned in Chapter 5.
2. *Ibid*. pp 86.

Chapter 7
1. Jung, C.G. *Psychology and Alchemy*. Routledge & Kegan Paul, 1975. p. 396.

Chapter Notes

2. Neumann, Eric. *The Great Mother*. p. 217. Quoting Kees.
3. Stanner, W.E.H. *White Man Got No Dreaming*. ANU Press, 1979 Cf. p. 26.
4. Origin. *Homily on Jeremiah*, 3,3. Quoted by Neumann.
5. See *The Mystery of the Serpent* in *The Mysteries* edited by Joseph Campbell. Bollingen Series XXX, 1955. p. 215.
6. *Ibid.* p. 215.
7. *Ibid.* Berndt. p. 36.
8. Warner, *A Black Civilization*.
9. Roheim, *The Eternal Ones of the Dream*.
10. See L.R. Hiat's article, *Swallowing and Regurgitation in Australian Myth and Rite* published in *Australian Aboriginal Mythology* for a comparative study of these ideas.
11. Affifi, A.E. *The Mystical Philosophy of Muhyid Din Ibnul Arabi*. Cambridge University Press, 1938. p. 114.
12. *Ibid.* Neumann. p. 55.
13. *Ibid.* The Mysteries. p. 218.
14. *Ibid*, p. 218.
15. Leisegang, Hans, *Die Gnosis*, Leipzig, 1936, p. 145.

Chapter 8
1. See Ananda Coomaraswamy's essay, *The Dance of Shiva. Fourteen Indian Essays*. Sagar Publications, New Delhi 1987.
2. Zimmer, Heinrich. *Philosophies of India*. Bollingen Series XXVI, 1974.
3. Budge, Wallace. *The Egyptian Book of the Dead*. Ch. CLIII. '...the deceased regarded it with horror and detestation. Every part of it — its poles and ropes, and weights and small cords, and hooks — had names which he was obliged to learn if he wished to escape from it.'
4. *Ibid.* Warner, p. 386.
5. Jung, C.G. and Kerényi, C., *Introduction to the Science of Mythology*. Routledge & Kegan Paul, 1951.
6. Layard, John, *Stone Men of Malekula*. London 1942.
7. Levy, Rachel. *The Gate of the Horn*, London 1948.
8. See Coomaraswamy's essay, *On the Loathly Bride*. Selected Papers Vol 1. Bollingen LXXXIX.
9. Jeremias, Alfred. *Der Antichrist in Geschichte und Gegenwart*. Leipzig, 1930. pp 4.
10. Hiatt, L.R. *Swallowing and Regurgitation in Australian Myth and Rite*. Australian Aboriginal Mythology.
11. Eliade, Mircea. *Myths, Dreams and Mysteries*. Fontana 1968.
12. *Ibid.* MDM p. 154.
13. *Ibid.* K p. 31.

14. Ibid. MDM p. 225.
15. Kerényi, C. *Hermes, Guide of Souls.* Spring Publications, Zurich, 1976.
16. *Ibid.* MDM 228.
17. *Ibid.* Hiatt, p. 156.
18. Jung, C.G. *Symbols of Transformation*, Routledge & Kegan Paul, 1956.

Part III: Among the Cloud Men

Chapter 9

1. A rain-maker's song calling upon a Wandjina not to deal falsely with him. The croaking sound of the last line is a gesture of sympathetic magic designed to induce rain by giving the sound of a frog that croaks when rain falls.
2. Grey, George. *Journals of Two Expeditions of Discovery*, 1841.
3. Elkin, A.P. *Rock-paintings of North-west Australia*, Oceania Vol 1, No. 3.
4. Capell, A. *Cave Painting Myths: Northern Kimberley*. Oceania Monograph No. 18, 1972.
5. *Ibid.* CPM p. 4.
6. Ezra Pound in Canto 74 (Faber 1973) wrote of the Wandjina:

> 'I am noman, my name is noman'
> but wanjina is, shall we say, Ouan Jin
> or the man with an education
> and whose mouth was removed by his father
> because he made too many *things*
> whereby he cluttered the bushman's baggage
> vide the expedition of Frobenius' pupils about
> 1938
>
> to Auss'ralia
> Ouan Jin spoke and thereby created the named
> thereby
> making clutter
> the bane of men moving
> and so his mouth was removed...

7. *Aenead*, Book VI.
8. Love, J.A.R. *Rock Paintings of the Worora and their Mythological Interpretation*. Journal of the Royal Society of Western Australia, Vol. 16, 1930. p.4.

Chapter Notes

9. See my *Mysteries of the Dreaming* (Prism Press) and *The Aborigine Tradition* (Element Books) for further information on totemism.
10. Elkin, A.P. *Totemism in North-Western Australia*. Oceania Vol. 3, No. 4 1933.
11. *Ibid*. TNA p. 470.
12. Compare Petronius: 'Each man makes his own dreams.'
13. Worms, E.A. *Contemporary and Prehistoric Rock Paintings*, pp. 549-550.
14. Elkin, A.P. *Grey's Northern Kimberley Cave-painting Re-found*. Oceania 19, Vol 4, 1948.
15. *The Elkin Papers* (unpublished) File 1/7/20, Box 24. Fisher Archives, University of Sydney. Under the Ganbowala myth.
16. *Ibid*. File 1/7/34.
17. See my *Messengers of the Gods*. (Bell Tower Books, 1993) for an exploration of the cave at Wanalirri.

Chapter 10
1. This myth is transcribed from the *Elkin Papers*. All the myths related in Part 3, except where otherwise stated, were collected by H. H. Coate on behalf of A.P. Elkin.

Chapter 11
1. Taittiriya Brahmana 2 .8. 8
2. Quoted by Zimmer, p. 72.
3. Quoted from a speech delivered by H.H. Coate based upon his linguistic research. Elkin Papers Box 29, file 1/7/85.
4. Elkin A.P. *Aboriginal Men of High Degree*. University of Queensland Press. p. 56.
5. Cf. St Thomas Aquinas, *Summa Theologica*: 'Knowledge comes about in so far as the object is within the knower.'
6. Abu Bakr ibn Tufail, *The Journey of a Soul*. Translated by Riad Kocache. The Octagon Press, 1985.

Chapter 12
1. Galaru's pronouncement to Djanara. *Ibid*. Capell p. 134.
2. Mountford, C.P. *Aboriginal Conception Beliefs*. Hyland House, 1981.
3. *Ibid*. Capell p. 117.
4. Eliade, Mircea. *Australian Religions*, Cornell University Press, 1977. Quoting Spencer and Gillan on the Aranda of Central Australia.
5. For further details on the making of a *barnmunji*, consult *Mysteries of the Dreaming*, Ch. 1, and *The Aborigine Tradition*, Ch. 6. Op. cit.
6. Coate, H.H. Unpublished manuscript, Elkin Papers. Box 24, 1/7/34.

7. *Ibid.* pp. 8-9.
8. Further elucidation on this subject can be found in *Messengers of the Gods*, Part 3. Bell Tower Books, 1993.

Conclusion
1. Otto, Rudolf. *Ibid.* p. 182.
2. Malinowski, B. *Myth in Primitive Psychology.* Kegan Paul, 1926.
3. Eliade, Mircea. *The Sacred and Profane.* New York, 1959. pp. 202 f.
4. Plutarch. *De Oraculorum defectu* (Mor. 419). Tr.Frank C. Babbitt (LCL, London 1936) pp. 401-2.
5. Otto, Walter. *Dionysus.* Spring Publications, 1981. p. 33.
6. Bourke, Johnson and White. *Before the Invasion. Aboriginal Life to 1788.* Oxford University Press, 1988. p. 51.

Bibliography

Berndt, R.M. - *The Eternal Ones of the Dream*. Oceania, Vol XVII, No.1
 - *Kunapipi*. Cheshire, 1951
 - *Djanggawul*. Routledge & Kegan Paul, 1952
 - *Sexual Behaviour in Western Arnhem Land*. Viking Publications in Anthropology, No.16, 1963
 - *The World of the First Australians*. (with C.H. Berndt) Ure Smith, 1977
Campbell, Joseph. — *The Mysteries*. (edit.) Bollingen, 1955
 - *The Hero with a Thousand Faces*. Bollingen, 1968
Capell, A. - *Cave Painting Myths: Northern Kimberley*. Oceania Monograph, 1972
Cassirer, Ernst. - *Language and Myth*. Dover Books, 1953
Coomaraswamy, A.K. — *The Dance of Shiva*. Sagar Publications, 1987
 - *The Transformation of Nature into Art*. Dover, 1956
 - *Traditional Art and Symbolism*. Bollingen, 1977
 - *Metaphysics*. Bollingen, 1977
Cowan, James. - *Mysteries of the Dreaming*. Prism Press, 1989
 - *The Aborigine Tradition*. Element Books, 1992
 - *Sacred Places*. Simon & Schuster, Sydney, 1991
 - *Letters from a Wild State*. Bell Tower, New York, 1992
 - *Messengers of the Gods*. Bell Tower, 1993
Crawford, I.M. *The Art of the Wandjina*. Oxford University Press, 1968
Eliade, Mircea. - *Myths, Dreams and Mysteries*. Fontana, 1968
 - *The Two and the One*. Harvill Press, 1965
 - *Aboriginal Religion*.
Elkin, A.P. - *Rock Paintings of North-West Australia*, Oceania Vol. I No. 3
 - *Studies in Australian Totemism*. Oceania Vol. III, No. 3 and 4
 - *Grey's Northern Kimberley cave-paintings refound*. Oceania Vol XIX, No.1
 - *Two Rituals in South and Central Arnhem Land*, Oceania Monograph, 19
 - *Aboriginal Men of High Degree*. University of Queensland Press, 1977
Godden, E. and Malnic, J. - *Rock Paintings of Aboriginal Australia*. Reed Books, 1982
Grey, George. - *Journal of Two Expeditions in North-Western Australia*. 2 vols. London, 1841
Jung, C.G. - *Alchemical Studies*. Routledge & Kegan Paul, 1967

181

Bibliography

- *Psychology and Alchemy*. Routledge & Kegan Paul, 1958
Kerényi, Karl. - *Athene*. Spring Publications, 1978
- *Introduction to the Science of Mythology* (with C.G. Jung). Routledge & Kegan Paul, 1951
- *The Gods of the Greeks*. Thames and Hudson, 1978
Kirk, G.S. - *Greek Myths* Pelican Books, 1974
Malinowski, B. *The Sexual Life of Savages*. Routledge & Kegan Paul, 1982
Massola, A. - *Bunjil's Cave. Myths, Legends and Superstitions of the Aborigines of South-east Australia*. Landsdowne Press, 1968
McConnel. U.H. *A Moon Legend from Bloomfield River, North Queensland*. Oceania Vol IV, No. 3
Meggitt, M.J. - *Gadjari among the Walbiri Aborigines of Central Australia*. Oceania Monograph No 14
Montagu, Ashley. *Coming into Being among the Australian Aborigines*. Routledge & Kegan Paul, 1974
Mountford, C.P. - *Ayers Rock*. Angus & Robertson, 1965
- *Winbaraku and the Myth of Jarapiri*. Rigby, 1968
- *Aboriginal Conception Beliefs*. Hyland House, 1988
Neumann, Eric. - *The Great Mother*. Bollingen, 1955
Otto, Rudolf - *The Idea of the Holy*. Oxford University Press, 1958
Otto, Walter F. - *The Homeric Gods*. Thames and Hudson, 1979
- *Dionysus*. Spring Books, 1981
Radcliffe-Brown, A.R., McConnel, A.R., Elkin, A.P. *The Rainbow Serpent...* Oceania, Vol 1, No. 3.
Robinson, Roland. *Aboriginal Myths and Legends*. Sun Books, 1977
Roughsey, D. - *Moon and Rainbow: the Autobiography of an Aboriginal*. A.H. and A.W. Reed, 1971
Santillana, G. *Hamlet's Mill*. David R. Godine, 1977
Spencer, B and Gillan F.J. - *The Native Tribes of Central Australia*. MacMillan, London 1899
- *Across Australia*. 2 vols. MacMillan, 1912
Stanner, W.E.H. *White Man Got No Dreaming*. Australian National University Press, 1979
Strehlow, T.G.H. - *Aranda Traditions*. Melbourne University Press, 1947
- *Songs of Central Australia*. Angus & Robertson, Sydney.
Versluis, Arthur - *Sacred Earth*. Inner Traditions, 1992
Von Brandenstein, C.G. - *Narratives from North-West of Western Australia*. Vols 1-3. Australian Aboriginal Studies, No. 35
- *Tararu. Aboriginal Song Poetry from the Pilbara*. Rigby, Adelaide.
Warner, L. - *A Black Civilization*. Harper, New York.
Zimmer, Heinrich -*The King and the Corpse*. Meridian Books, 1960
- *Myths and Symbols in Indian Art and Civilization*. Bollingen, 1974
- *Philosophies of India*. Bollingen, 1974

INDEX

Index

Index

Layard, John 100
Levi-Strauss 91

MacDonnell Ranges 9, 21
Malinowski, B. 165-6
man of high degree 155
man of knowledge 18, 65, 141; *and see* mekigar
manduwul 118
marriage, ritual 95, 101
meditation 121, 144
mekigar 38
Muruwul 73-8, 80-4; *and see* waterhole, sacred
myth, Christian 15, 23, 42, 153
myth, classical 27, 28, 47, 48, 49, 53-5, 119, 135
myth, creation of *see* mythogenesis
myth, destruction of 10, 18
myth, enactment of 28-9, 59, 169-70, 172
myth, identification with 12, 20, 167
myth, merging of 66
myth, modern 171
myth of Ankotarinja 25-7, 35ff
myth of Creation *see* Ankotarinja
myth of Djangawul 66-7
myth of humankind *see* Wauwalak Sisters
myth of Nangina 127-35, 137ff
myth of Wauwalak Sisters 73-8, 87ff, 97ff
myth, reverence of 13, 54, 66
myth, role of 1, 5, 164, 166
myth, two versions of 30
myth, universal cultures of 3, 14, 36, 47, 165
myth, unravelling of 17-19
myth *v.* science 11-12, 163
mythic landscape 9, 11, 18, 19, 58-9, 70-1
mythic heroes, world-ordering by 28
mythic heroes, transformation of 39, 42-3
mytho-history 4
mythogenesis, language of 4, 29-30, 104, 163ff
mythogenesis 10-12, 14, 44, 96, 122, 164

Namanjolk 15
Nangina 12ff, 165
Neumann, E. 93
Ngalenga *see* myth of Nangina

Index

Nietzsche 163
nongaru 65, 69, 85, 103, 107
novice *see* iliara

Old Woman *see* Kunapipi
Otto, Rudolf 165
Otto, Walter 30, 168, 169

Parr Erultja 26-7, 87; *and see* Ankotarinja
Philosophic Tree 39
Pound, Ezra 41
power-centre, sacred 121, 122, 151, 156

rain-making 48, 55, 99, 118
Rainbow Serpent 15, 19, 48, 63, 65, 69, 90, 158
Rainbow Serpent (contd) *and see* Galaru; Great Snake; Julungul
rebirth *see* death-and-rebirth
Red Centre *see* Australia, Central
reincarnation *see* death-and-rebirth
repainting, significance of 118, 122
Rg Veda 36, 52, 58, 68, 85, 94, 140
Ripley, Sir George 87
ritual activity *see* body painting; dance; sacrifice; song
ritual environment *see* nongaru
rock painting 1, 19, 64, 116, 121, 138, 144-5; *and see* dot-art
Roheim 92
rubbish country 17

sacrifice, ritual 107
sacrifice, significance of 52, 55-7, 79, 89, 105-6, 135, 159
Satapatha Brahmana 37, 41, 56, 57
settlement, early 9-10, 67
Simon of Taibutheh 135
song 1, 10, 18, 28, 29, 30, 73, 79-80, 105, 118, 154 *and see* Kunapipi, songs of
songman 15, 30, 57, 80
spirit-child 151, 152
spirit-entity 15, 18, 19, 117, 169, 172; Eaglehawk; Galaru; Kunapipi; Namanjolk; Nangina; Rainbow Serpent; Ungud; Wauwalak Sisters; *and see* Ankotarinja; Djangawul;
spirit-entity, contact with 169
spirit-mark 9
spirit-path *see* manduwul
Strehlow, T.G.H. 21-2, 28, 50

186

Index